D1296100

THE THIRD ALTERNATIVE:
CHRISTIAN SELF-GOVERNMENT

FREEDOM WITHOUT ANARCHY
ORDER WITHOUT TYRANNY
PEACE AND PROSPERITY

By Bill Burtness
With Patrick Butler

xulon PRESS

Copyright © 2003 by Bill Burtness

THE THIRD ALTERNATIVE: Christian Self-government
Freedom without Anarchy, Order without Tyranny, Peace and
Prosperity
by Bill Burtness

Printed in the United States of America

ISBN 1-591602-32-7

All rights reserved. No part of this publication may be reproduced
or transmitted in any form or by any means without written permis-
sion of the publisher.

Unless otherwise indicated, Bible quotations are taken from the
New American Standard Bible, Copyright © 1971 by The Lockman
Foundation.

Xulon Press
www.XulonPress.com

Xulon Press books are available in bookstores everywhere, and on
the Web at www.XulonPress.com.

ACKNOWLEGEMENTS

I remember sitting dumbfounded! My wife, Susan, and I were attending a three month long seminar concerning renewal and the different problems facing America and the world. For 10 weeks, we had studied about Socialism, Humanist education, conspiracy, occult in the schools, pornography, Communism, etc. and had all but totally lost hope. Then Miss Verna Hall and Miss Rosalie Slater from the Foundation for American Christian Education stood and began the final two weeks of teaching with the statement, "In the next two weeks we will show you <u>how</u> to rebuild the United States of America." I remember sitting dumfounded!

But that is exactly what they did! The hope for the future they imparted to us based on the finished work of Christ and the sovereignty of God has transformed my life with purpose. I would like to gratefully acknowledge their gift of practical wisdom and vision. Miss Hall's <u>The Christian History of the Constitution of the United States of America</u> and Miss Slater's <u>Teaching and Learning America's Christian History</u> and their other works are monumental stockpiles of research for blessing the next generation with purpose and hope.

I'm most grateful to my wife, Susan, for her intelligence, practical additions and editorial help. We have hammered out much of this work on the anvil of shared experience. And our four kids, Rachael, Rebekah, John and Mark have been the fruitful proving ground of God's kingdom. And to our son-in-law, the husband of daughter Rachael, Matt Piercey, for his continual encouragement and the www.JudahBible.com website.

I want to also acknowledge my parents, Roger and Kathryn Burtness, my grandmother, Mrs. Grace Burtness, and my parents-in-law, Barton and Arlene Siebring, for all their prayers, support, concern and love for us.

Many thanks to Mrs. Ruth Smith of the Pilgrim Institute in Granger, Indiana, who made the concepts and ideas more easily understood and practical with her seminars on "Rudiments of America's Christian History, Government and Education."

I would like to acknowledge the late Mr. Harry Conn and the late Mr. Gordon C. Olson for their in-depth understanding of the grace of God and how to build strong individual Christian character, which is the only basis for liberty.

I especially want to thank Loren and Darlene Cunningham and the rest of our Youth with a Mission (YWAM) friends and leaders for their vision for world evangelism and the countless hours of teaching, counsel, and vision with which they have blessed us.

I also want to acknowledge Mr. Russ Walton for his basic understanding of the thread of God's purpose and the unfolding of His government through the Bible. I also want to thank Jim and Barbara Kilkenny and John and Suzanne Hunter of YWAM and Christian Heritage School in Tyler, Texas, for all the hours we've spent brainstorming and praying about changing the world with our Lord Jesus.

I would like to thank Dr. Paul and Mrs. Jessie Yardy for their invaluable teaching applying the Scriptures to the area of raising children. We are forever indebted to them for their practical, Biblical wisdom.

I would like also to thank Patrick Butler of the University of the Nations, Woodcrest campus, for his creativity and help in the style and readability of this book, and his continual encouragement for the project.

I am eternally grateful to the Lord Jesus who saved my soul, saved my marriage, saved my life, saved my future, and teaches me each day how to love God with all my heart and soul and mind and strength.

DEDICATION

This book is dedicated to my wonderful wife Susan. As the committed mother of our four children, she has taught me all about faithfulness, loyalty and deferring present gratification for future fulfillment.

TABLE OF CONTENTS

CHAPTER I.

THE THIRD ALTERNATIVE

God is Sovereign.

"**W**hat can my nation do?"

A tall African man stood up in the audience to ask me this question.

I was in the middle of a lecture on the Lordship of Christ and World Missions. He was from Nigeria. I am from Illinois, U.S.A., where I was giving the lecture at a college Sunday school class at the University of Illinois.

We appraised each other through a vast grid of culture, language, experience and distance. Our common bond was Christ. The year was 1977 and he posed the question I will never forget.

"What can my nation do?" he said with a beautiful Nigerian accent. "In Nigeria we are sixty percent Christians. Yet our society is characterized by chaos, tyranny, gross ignorance and abject poverty. What can my nation do?"

The facts he presented astonished me. "Sixty percent Christians!" I thought. Even though I believed that the Gospel would have a positive effect on any culture, I really hadn't a clue how to solve his problem. I heard myself say something to the effect of, "Just trust the Lord, brother." It sounded so hollow and meaningless to me.

It must have sounded that way to him, too, because his face suddenly became anguished as if he'd been punched in the chest. He sat down in more pain than when he stood.

At that moment I was devastated by my own ignorance and shallowness, and my inability to give that man *any* hope. It seemed like I was saying, "Depart in peace. Be warmed and filled," (James

2:16). That very day I began to pray in earnest, "Lord Jesus, what *can* his nation do? Surely You have answers. Surely Your word has answers. Surely there must be hope. But I don't see it. Lord, what *can* his nation do?"

In answer to that prayer, the Lord began to bring across my path individuals, seminars, teachers and resources that shed light on this new heart-cry of mine.

At the same time, as an American believer in Jesus Christ, I have been distressed by the downward cultural slide of my own nation, noticeable in my own short lifetime. The questions in the back of my mind have been, "Why is this happening?" and "How can it be redressed?" Many are blinded to this slide by external success and momentary material prosperity. My question now is, "Lord, what can *my* nation do?"

After being raised from the dead, Jesus gave His followers a last command, a great commission, before his ascension:

> And Jesus came up to [His disciples] and said, "All authority in heaven and on earth has been given to Me. Go ye therefore and make disciples of all the nations, baptizing them in the name of the Father and of the Son and of the Holy Spirit, teaching them to do all that I have commanded you. And lo, I am with you always, even to the end of the age." Matt. 28:18-19

The 20th century has seen a vast increase in going and baptizing, in international missions and planting churches.

In our own day, there is now also a renewed emphasis on discipling and teaching the nations. This means we believers taking seriously our responsibility as stewards of our societies, moving beyond the doorways of our churches to apply Biblical principles to every aspect of life. The purpose of this is so that our societies and cultures can shift towards freedom, order and prosperity from tyranny, chaos and suffering. Part of this discipleship has to do with government.

If we are going to disciple the nations, we are going to have to understand the Biblical philosophy of government.

This book is intended to be a layman's primer on the personal moral (internal) and structural (external) foundations of a free society. It is not an exhaustive treatise. It is an introduction to the basics, a beginning point, much of which was left out of our own education. There are many resources available by authors past and present for further study, but everyone must understand and implement the basics or we are doomed to tyranny.

The world is crying out for liberty. As the Soviet Communist tyranny unraveled in Eastern Europe, the result was economic collapse, civil war and bloodshed. Many had thought it would mean freedom and peace and prosperity! Why did we suppose that? From where does liberty come? Is liberty simply the absence of tyranny? Is liberty license to do what "I want?" Is democracy itself the answer? Can liberty be sustained? How is liberty sustained? Is God in control? How? Is there hope?

These are questions that we as Christians must be able to answer in order to communicate the reality of the kingdom of God to others effectively, keep the freedoms we have and help the nations we are serving reap the blessings that God desires for them. Social reform is part of loving our neighbors as ourselves.

THE THIRD ALTERNATIVE

Eroded as they are, American political institutions are rooted in the Biblical philosophy of <u>Christian Self-government</u> where political sovereignty rests in the individual under God rather than in either the state or the church on the one hand, or the individual in and of himself on the other. Christian self-government is the third alternative. In other words the state is not God and the individual is not God, but God is God. In order for these institutions to work as they should, the individual must understand how to govern himself under God in every area of life including the civil sphere, delegating proper authority to his public representatives. Otherwise he will delegate improper authority, actively or passively, and will end up losing his freedom.

We are bombarded daily by various <u>issues</u> from economics to "family values," but what are the Biblical <u>principles</u> that define the issues and provide guidance and solutions to the problems of society?

This book is written to address the need for a basic understanding of the principles of Christian self-government and their application. It will show from the Bible how God changes nations. The application of these principles in *any* nation will release and protect liberty without spawning chaos.

Learning these principles will help us recognize the hand of God in our lives, our nation and our world, and help us interpret the news and current events from His perspective. Seeing the providence of God gives needed hope for the future. Seeing the crucial significance of all our efforts in God's kingdom gives needed courage to "be steadfast, immovable, always abounding in the work of the Lord, knowing that [our] toil is not in vain in the Lord," (I Cor. 15:58).

This book is also intended to show the necessity of personal reconciliation to God through Jesus Christ, which besides being God's greatest desire and the individual's only hope for eternity, is the cornerstone of a free society as well. It also points out the crucial need for true Spiritual awakening, prayerful evangelism, loving discipleship, and Biblical Christian education as the source of our social action and decisions.

It must be clarified that this book is not about politics but about government. The dictionary definition of "politics" is "factional scheming for power and status within a group, sometimes crafty or unprincipled" (Webster's New World Dictionary). This aspect is distasteful to Christians and can cause us to shy away from the subject of government altogether. Our discussion here, however, will not focus on politics but on philosophy of government.

"An exciting book on government is what we need!" Though this seems to be a contradiction in terms, it is only oxymoronic if we leave out the Governor. He is the most exciting Being in the universe and governing is His forte. Who He is, what He does, how He does it and why He does it comprise the study of government.

TENDENCIES TODAY

Concerning the civil sphere of government, in our day in America, Christians seem to fall prey to two errors in thought. The first is the thinking that civil government *as an institution* is at enmity with God, that civil government is the enemy of the church. This stems from the thought that civil government is man's idea, which is an evolutionary notion and is how the world naturally thinks, not believing in God's existence. As a result, civil government barely enters the consciousness of Christians. Many believers subconsciously think, "What do I have to do with civil government?" and in the extreme, "The non-Christians will take care of civil government. It's their domain." Since Christians are also usually busy with family, church, jobs or helping their neighbor, civil government often slides to the bottom of the list of priorities. Many, perhaps most, Christians don't bother to vote, much less take an active part in the political process.

The consequence of this mentality is that the majority of people involved in civil government are those motivated by self-interest rather than love and the highest good. Even though we pray for Godly government, only the ungodly are actually involved. The result is that power shifts upwards to the state and freedom evaporates. Christians are surprised that abortion becomes legal, condoms are distributed in schools and evangelism becomes outlawed as "religious discrimination," and even a "hate crime." But this should be no surprise considering the fallen state of men. The ungodly are doing what the ungodly naturally do, acting from within their limited worldview.

There comes a reaction to this predicament, in which Christians fall into the second error of thought, which is control. The thinking goes, "*We* must control society to prevent and redress this downward slide and loss of freedom!" Notice the contradiction. This is also a move towards tyranny, the difference being in *who* will control, the ungodly or the Christians. This thinking gives rise to a so-called "Christian Right" which perhaps justifiably strikes fear into the hearts of many and produces violent reaction to the church.

But God's way is neither apathy nor control, but love. Love is defined as an active laboring for the highest good of all, and its ways and means are expounded by God in the Bible. The Bible shows us that civil government *as an institution* is not at enmity with God, but is an institution ordained and given by God, with certain specific purposes. As such, Christians are the stewards of civil government as an aspect of their stewardship of society. Our job is to keep civil government within the boundaries that God has set for it, which are protecting the individual and controlling the evil. As believers abandon this stewardship, the ungodly rise to fill the vacuum, corruption and perversion ensue, the individual is controlled and the evil is protected! This is why believers often seem to be on the wrong side of civil government, which in turn propagates the sense that civil government is not our business.

The major cause of the decline of our civil structure in America is ultimately found to be a lack of Godly Biblical character on the part of Christians. On the one hand, this lack of character manifests itself in an apathy that does not recognize Jesus' command to "Occupy till I come" (Luke 19:13), and does not spend time, energy and resources exercising stewardship in the area of civil government. On the other hand, this lack surfaces as a "worldly spirit" that seeks to control people rather than help them. Controlling is easier than helping.

Civil government as an institution ordained by God is a concept difficult to recognize because governments are staffed by people, and considering man's nature is fallen, the above mentioned corruption and perversion of God's purpose for civil government are pervasive.

FIX THE PROBLEMS

There are two other divine institutions that God has given to mankind: the Family whose purpose is nurture, and the Church whose purpose is provision, spiritual, social and physical. Similar problems are seen within these institutions as we note in civil government. Families are "staffed" with people. Many are "staffed" with the ungodly and are filled with corruption, violence and perversion of God's purpose of nurture. Yet Christians don't say that the family is at enmity with God and should therefore be abolished. It is the world who sees the corruption and concludes that the family is obsolete and should be abandoned. The proper response is, "No, the family as an institution is a divine institution with a divine purpose, and we need to fix it and bring it back to that purpose of nurture."

If civil government is a divine institution with a divine purpose, then obviously that purpose has been and is continually being perverted. As God's stewards, we Christians have been sluggards. It is our responsibility from God to fix the problems and restore civil government to its proper Biblical purpose. This is a long-term labor on various fronts, not simply gaining control in the next election and relaxing. It will take a depth of character that we as the body of Christ have been lacking. Shifting power downwards which increases liberty, i.e. decentralizing power, means taking on the corresponding responsibility at the individual level, whether in education, welfare, economics, crime or the environment.

The good news is that the church in America is growing in character and in understanding the ways of God. In chapters to come, we will discuss the Biblical philosophy of government, the basis and purpose of the institution of civil government, the connection between liberty and individual character, and the personal application of these principles in the various spheres of life. We will see how every one of us Christians can effectively exercise our God-given stewardship of society, particularly in the area of civil government.

CHAPTER II.

THE SOURCE OF LIBERTY

The link between character and freedom.

In 14th century England, Oxford University professor and Bible scholar John Wycliffe concluded from his study of the Bible that if the people of a society would govern their own lives, rejecting wrong and doing right voluntarily, there would be no need for a government of external force to control them. "Dominion belongs to grace," he said. By this he meant that dominion, or top authority, which at that time was a government of external force that depended on the sword to control the people, would ultimately yield to a government of moral principle controlling the people. He saw placing the Bible in the hands of the people as the means to accomplish this change in government. The people could then read the Bible, come to know God personally through Jesus Christ, and reform their lives in accordance with Biblical principles in every area: personal, family, ecclesiastical, and finally civil and economic. In fact, with respect to civil government Wycliffe said, "This Bible is for the government of the people, by the people, for the people."[1] He concluded that the source of liberty in a society is widespread individual Christian character.

Thus Wycliffe believed that placing the Bible in the hands of the people would ultimately topple the tyrannies of Europe, and that this was the only means to bring about this change. These ideas impelled him to translate the Bible into common English, and his followers taught people to read so they could study, understand and apply it. As these ideas began to echo throughout Europe, a reformation movement was ignited that changed the course of history.

The existence of liberty depends on understanding and applying the Biblical philosophy of government: Christian self-government. To restore liberty then, we must first gain a proper understanding. As our culture has become secularized, we have not been taught the basic principles of Christian self-government in our schools. Nor have our churches taught us. The first problem we must overcome, then, is ignorance. The second factor is application, or a willingness to actually do what the Bible tells us in every sphere of life. In the United States, those affected by the revival movements of the 1960's and 1970's have been learning Christian self-government in the personal sphere, the family and the ecclesiastical sphere. Other spheres of life, which are just beginning to be reformed, are education, economics, civil government, the arts and the media.

Education is key in God's plan, and the Christian school movement and the Christian homeschool movement are encouraging signs of His hand at work. We must be careful that in our Christian homes, schools and churches we are building Biblical character in the next generation that can create and sustain liberty rather than dependent character.

We see the crucial need for this Biblical kind of character in the Commonwealth of Independent States (CIS), the former Soviet Union, where the character of the people has been trained for generations to be dependent on the state for provision, direction and control. One saying in the CIS is, "They have given us freedom and taken away our food!" This expresses a character of dependence on the state. Similarly, this is what the sons of Israel said when confronted with the necessity of governing themselves under God in the wilderness after being raised in ancient Egypt with a mentality of dependence on the state:

> "...and also the sons of Israel wept again and said, 'Who will give us meat to eat? We remember the fish that we used to eat free in Egypt, the cucumbers and the melons and the leeks and the onions and the garlic, but now our appetite is gone. There is nothing to look at but this manna.'" Num. 11:4-6

The fact of the matter was that the fish and the leeks and onions were not free! The people paid for them with their whole lives in servitude to the state. Now, instead of depending on the state for food, they needed to depend on God, gather the manna themselves and be content and thankful for His provision. Individually they had to govern their attitudes and tongues, a very difficult task, and take the initiative to gather food for themselves each day. They felt it had been easier in Egypt.

The Biblical philosophy of government is Christian self-government, or self-government under God. Let us define each of these terms.

Throughout this book, when speaking of God with a capital "G" we are referring to the personal infinite God of the Bible whose character is unrelenting love and faithfulness. The Bible reveals that it is this God who created the heavens and the earth. He created man in His image. When men chose rebellion instead of love as their purpose in life, God responded in love. Ultimately, God became a man in Jesus Christ to show us what love is, to die for our sins and to rise from the dead for our personal salvation. God offers this salvation from sin equally to everyone on condition of repentance and faith.

The term "government" refers to "the flow of power which controls the actions of the individual." To govern is simply to control or regulate.[2] An individual's actions are controlled or governed by various things. Generally, the term "government" brings into our minds a picture of the dome-shaped building in our national or state capitol, but that represents only one aspect or sphere of government - civil government. There are other spheres of government as well: family, church, classroom, etc. We will be using the term "government" in the general sense of "that which controls the actions of the individual" and will identify specific spheres of government as needed.

The term "Christian" is important in that it identifies the basis of this government as the Bible and the ruler of this government as Christ Jesus reigning in the heart of the individual. Without this absolute anchor, "Christian self-government" is reduced to only "self government" where each individual decides for himself how to govern his life and the values to which he will cling. This exercise of individual autonomy is exactly what occurred in the book of

Judges as the sons of Israel, freed from the external tyranny of Egypt, slid away from individual relationship with God and obedience to His Law of Love. The last words of Judges describe this chaos: "In those days there was no king in Israel; everyone did what was right in his own eyes," (Judg. 21:24). Pharaoh was not their king and God was no longer their king either. The result was terrible anarchy: freedom without order. The book of Judges is so violent that one may wonder why it is included in the Bible! But it is a frank chronicle of what happens when a free people turns its liberty to license as it drifts from God.

The term "self" refers to the individual's responsibility to make right choices and obey God's law on his own. Without this term we have only "Christian government," which would be an external form of tyranny based on Biblical law. We do have in the world today civil governments that are external tyrannies based on religious law, some even derived from the Pentateuch. This, however, is externally imposed order without freedom.

In America generally, Bible-believing Christians recognize that something in our society is terribly wrong and needs to be corrected, that we have strayed far from Biblical values and are reaping the consequences. Many of these sincere Christian Americans feel, as do many other Americans, that the civil government needs to fix these problems. These Christians reason, "If we can elect only Christians to public office and implement Biblical law, we will have righteousness. We will be a Christian nation. Then we can relax." In fact, however, the result would just be a Christian tyranny. This is a call for greater governmental control of the people, "Christian Socialism." It indicates a character of dependence on external structure and is reflective of a shift among Christians across the ecclesiastical spectrum from individual dependence on God and the Bible to dependence on man and society. This is why we need revival. God's way is not tyranny, even Biblical tyranny, but liberty.

The Biblical philosophy of government is that the individual is to govern his own life according to God's law and do what is right voluntarily. The civil government, then, is created not to control the individual but to protect his freedom and safety, to protect him from those who refuse to govern themselves: "a terror to evil and a servant for good" (Rom. 13:3-4). The challenge is to <u>keep</u> the civil government in its proper place. Thus, there can be freedom <u>and</u> order. Yet this combination is dependent on the people controlling themselves. To this extent liberty is voluntary. This is government by moral principle supplanting government by force.

Is this possible?

To understand the Biblical philosophy of government (again, not civil government) there are two aspects we must study:

1) the source of government

2) our view of sovereignty

TWO SOURCES OF GOVERNMENT

The question arises, "Where does this flow of power that controls the individual's actions come from?" There are actually two sources of government. One source is internal and the other source is external. Government comes either from within or from without.

The first source of government is <u>internal</u>. This refers to the individual's actions being governed by the reign of the Lord Jesus in his heart. The individual is submitted to the Lordship of Jesus Christ, and is voluntarily controlled. The Bible refers to this as the kingdom of God. Internal government is not the individual doing anything he wants; that is license. Rather, the individual is doing what is right on his own. God's law provides for this government an absolute base.

The term "kingdom of God" is a term that arose in the 400-year period between the Old and New Testaments. It is not found in the Old Testament. By the time Jesus came there were various ideas of what the kingdom of God would be. Prevalent among them was the vision that the coming Messiah would muster His army, ride into Jerusalem, overthrow the pagan and unjust Romans, set up His kingdom in the land, and cause the sons of Israel to live in peace, safety and increasing grandeur forever.

Isaiah had prophesied many years before about the Messiah, saying,

> "For a child will be born to us, a son will be given
>   to us;

And the government will rest on His shoulders;
And His name will be called Wonderful Counselor,
    Mighty God, Eternal Father, Prince of Peace.
There will be no end to the increase of His
    government or of peace,
On the throne of David and over His kingdom,
To establish it and to uphold it with justice and
    righteousness
From then on and forevermore." Is. 9:6-7

But Jesus came preaching repentance, saying, "Repent for the kingdom of God is at hand!" (Matt. 4:17) Repentance from sin to righteousness was central to this new kingdom. When asked by his disciples how to pray, Jesus said to pray "Thy kingdom come, Thy will be done on earth as it is in heaven," (Matt. 6:10). Doing the will of God was characteristic of this new kingdom. God's kingdom, then, is not an external political kingdom like the kingdoms of the world. The King of this new kingdom declared Himself after His resurrection, when Jesus said to His disciples, "All authority in heaven and on earth has been given unto Me," (Matt. 28:18). Authority had been taken from the devil and given to Jesus (Phil. 2:9-11). "Now is the ruler of this world cast out," (John 12:31). Jesus instructed His disciples to "Go, make disciples of all the nations" (Matt. 28:19), and "Go into all the world and preach this good news to every creature," (Mark 16:15). The authority of Satan and the power of sin had been broken.

The result, or consequence, of this new internal kingdom of Jesus reigning in the hearts of individuals is liberty. "Where the Spirit of the Lord is there is liberty," (II Cor. 3:17). First, of course, is internal liberty (Rom. 6:16-18). Jesus frees us from the power of sin and from guilt, to righteousness, being governed by love, and dependence on God instead of man. The effect of this internal liberty of soul is external liberty in society, as Biblical choices are made to secure the highest good in every area of life.

The second source of government is external. This refers to the control of the individual's actions by external things such as the state, the church, circumstances, fears, lusts, and guilt rather than active choice. External government arises in the absence of being controlled internally by Jesus and being submitted to Him. The other kingdom besides God's kingdom is the Devil's kingdom, where Jesus does not reign in the heart of the individual (Col. 1:13, John 12:31, Rom. 6:16), but the individual is enslaved to sin and self, resulting in death. He is governed by fear instead of love. As he does not recognize the reality of God and His kingdom, whether by not recognizing His existence (non-Christian) on the one hand, or by not submitting to His lordship (nominal Christian) on the other, he grows dependent on man instead of on God. The consequence of this dependence on man becomes dependence on the state, which gives rise to the "kingdoms of this world" (John 18:36). As people depend more and more on the state, they give more power to the state. The state inevitably becomes increasingly corrupt, multiplying the misery.

God's first commandment to us is that we should have no other gods besides Him. The reason for this command is that He is the only one who will "never fail us nor will He ever forsake us" (Heb. 13:5). He is the only one worthy of our complete dependence, allegiance, trust and love. Anything or anyone else that we depend upon, whether possessions or self or others or the church or the state, will ultimately fail us, disappoint us and break our hearts. God loves us and does not want our hearts broken, and gave us this Law for our protection. The world is full of disappointed, disillusioned and embittered people, even Christians, whose trust and dependence have been misdirected from Jesus to an unworthy substitute.

To illustrate the difference between being internally and externally governed, I often mention in lectures that I do not steal cars. I ask the audience to speculate on why I do not steal cars. Typically the first answer out is "Because you might get caught!"

Actually, fear of being caught is not why I do not steal cars. The reason I don't steal cars is because it is wrong. I have come to see that my sin grieves the heart of God because of its destructive power on my relationship with Him, on myself, and on others. The guilt caused by doing what we know is wrong distorts all our relationships. Yet God so loved the world that He sent His only begotten Son Jesus to die for me so that I could be reconciled to God and have that personal relationship with Him restored (John 3:16). Sin has cost God more than I can imagine, yet He loves me. While I was still a sinner, He loved me and intervened in my life with mercy to save me from my self and my sin (Rom. 5:5). As I have come to know Him, I have grown in His attitude toward sin: hatred for sin in my own life and grief over sin in others' lives. It is because of His love for me that I don't steal cars, or anything else for that matter. I want to please Him, not grieve Him. In this way "The love of Christ controls us," (II Cor. 5:14). Fear of being caught is an external motivation.

The point here is that I am internally governed in that area of my life - stealing. Hopefully I am growing in internal government in <u>all</u> areas of my life. Now, there are those who are not internally governed in this area of their lives, but only externally governed. A few years ago, a riot broke out in Los Angeles when four policemen were acquitted of brutality. Whether the verdict was good or bad, the ensuing chaos was of sufficient magnitude to render the police force, the externally governing structure, ineffective. Without the external control, many who were only externally governed in the area of stealing went out and looted the stores. When asked "Why?" only a very few looters said they were there in protest of the verdict. Most said "I wanted a couch," or "Because it's fun," or "Because everyone else is doing it." The verdict, then, did not actually spark the looting, but rather became an excuse for lawlessness. The real problem was the character of the people, not the lack of policemen, internal not external. Afterwards, city leaders were asking, "How can we be better prepared in the future?" However, greater external force (tyranny) is not the real answer, but greater internal control. We need a new spiritual awakening to restore Godly character in America. "In those days there was *no* authority in Los Angeles, each one did what was right in his own eyes."

We must add that there are also those who are not even externally controlled in the area of stealing cars, but are uncontrolled. Threat of punishment is not a controlling force for them and they steal cars anyway.

Jesus' kingdom is one in which Jesus has come into an individual's life, has freed him from his guilt from the past, is changing his heart by His love to appreciate and obey righteousness and is preparing him for eternity. One of the fruits of the Holy Spirit is self-control (Gal. 5:23). The controlling power of the love of Jesus on the individual's actions is greater than any externally governing force. One would think the threat of horrible death by AIDS would control people's actions, but it does not.

Jesus points out that "Unless you are born again, you cannot see the kingdom of God," (John 3:3). Without a real and personal relationship with God through Jesus Christ, the possibility of this internal motivation and control does not exist. There is only external control, whether by police or military force, psychological manipulation, or educational or media indoctrination. This gives the state or the psychological, educational, and media elites the driving and crushing sense that it is up to them to control the people and provide salvation.

BOTH INTERNAL AND EXTERNAL GOVERNMENT

Here on earth, both internal and external government are at work at all times in any society, whether a nation, a family, or even a classroom. In Fig. 2.1, the dark outer circle represents the total government needed in a society to control the actions of the individual, and is constant. This is divided into the internal component and the external component. The internal component represents the character of the people and the external component refers to the force applied from without to control the people.

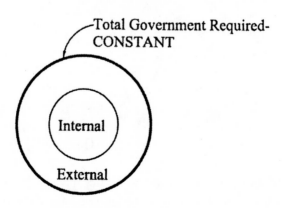

Fig. 2.1 Components Of Government.

In this diagram, as the strength of character increases and the people govern themselves to do what is right voluntarily, the area within the inner circle representing the component of internal control increases. The area representing external force gets smaller, signifying an increase in liberty. As individual character increases, liberty increases.

On the other hand, as the people fall away from God, and Godly character decreases in the society, the area representing internal government gets smaller and the area representing external force increases, signifying evaporating freedom and a move towards tyranny. A decline in individual character brings about a decline in liberty.

We can see the ultimate end of this by extrapolating to eternity. The Bible says there will be a day when those who have chosen righteous relationship with God and those who have chosen unrighteousness and selfishness will be separated, each going to the place he has chosen, to heaven or hell. God will allow those who do not want to be with Him forever to go to a place where He is not! We know that those who do not want Him here are certainly not going to want Him there.

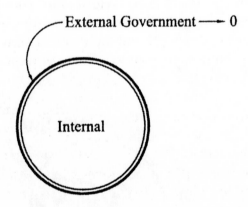

Fig. 2.2 Heaven.

In heaven, everyone will be internally governed by Jesus through love. There will be no need for external force to control their actions because they will be doing what they want to do, doing what is right and the highest good. They will be doing what they love. There will be order yet liberty. The consequence will be peace and freedom *because of* the character of the people there in love relationship with God. It will be heaven! And it will last forever.

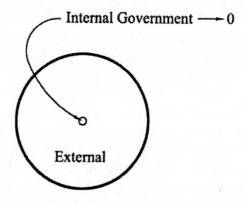

Fig. 2.3 Hell.

On the other hand, those in hell will be there because they do not want to govern their lives according to God's law of love, but are living for their own personal happiness and advancement as their purpose in life. They never repented of those motives to live for Jesus. Soon after judgement day (1000 years?) all vestige and memory of God, love, righteousness, compassion, and mercy will be gone and the internal component of government will have disappeared, leaving only external government. It will be total chaos in absolute slavery, ruled in terror by Satan and his angels (Matt. 25:41), who, of course wrote the book on corruption. It will be hell! And it will last forever. But it was chosen.

A mini-society that illustrates this situation would be a prison. Those incarcerated are there because they do not govern themselves according to righteousness. They are now governed externally by the State in an absolute way.

Another example with which many can identify is this. When I was first in college, I would generally study for my exams the night before the exam. Many times I stayed up all night cramming, and walked into the exam red-eyed and exhausted. I had not governed myself to study daily, and now there came "weeping and gnashing of teeth." In this case I was externally governed by fear of failing the exam.

On one occasion, I <u>had</u> to pass the exam but I had not studied. So, the day before the exam, I actually chained myself to my desk. I gave the key to my roommate who would check on me every so often. In this sense, slavery or bondage is voluntary - the individual being dependent on external government due to a refusal to govern self, or a lack of internal government. Ultimately this did not work. Starting over at another college later, I learned new study habits, governing myself to keep up each day. Exam day was just another class; I reviewed a little and did reasonably well on the test. There was peace and freedom when I took on the responsibility.

Of the two sources of government, the internal component is the cause and the external component is the effect. The character of the people is the cause and the external structure is the effect. In a family, that which defines how much freedom a parent will give his teenager is the child's ability to govern himself (activities, curfew, etc.) according to the parent's requirements. In a nation, the amount or strength of external civil government and its structure is defined by the ability of the people to govern their own lives under God in every area. In this sense, people get the government they deserve, or more succinctly the government their character requires. So the answer to the world's political problems and chaos is the gospel of Jesus Christ and godly character. This is more than raising one's hand in a church service for salvation, but actual repentance and becoming internally governed in every area of life. As internal government is strengthened, external government can release liberty, civil and economic, without risking chaos. This is usually not without a fight, however, because people in power don't like to let it slip away.

The story is told of the great Russian author Alexander Solzhenitsyn and his grandson walking and discussing the decay of the Russian political and natural landscape. His grandson asked, "What happened?" Solzhenitsyn's answer was, "We have forgotten God." This is a warning to us in the West that individually we must not forget God if our civilization is to continue to prosper in liberty. We are at a dangerous decision point as a civilization at this time. Moses gave the sons of Israel this stern warning:

"And it shall come about if you ever forget the

Lord your God, and go after other gods and serve them and worship them, I testify against you today that you shall surely perish." Deut. 8:19

It is astonishing, yet true, that most of the world's suffering is caused directly by sin. The rest is caused indirectly by sin. As we have also seen, the slavery in the world is caused by sin. So the way to alleviate the slavery and the suffering is to work against the sin! Our relief efforts are needed, but they do not touch the cause of the problem unless they are accompanied by the gospel of Jesus Christ. For example, there are many starving in India. The problem, however, is not a lack of food, but that the people are not able to buy the food. The problem is economic. In fact, India is a food-exporting nation. Economic stagnation is the result of political stagnation. The problem is also a religious problem. Rats are eating the food in storage. But the people worship the rats and will not exterminate them. The way to eliminate starvation in India is to proclaim the gospel of Jesus Christ. The Bible shows that there is a difference in value between people and rats.

I once asked a missionary friend to the Machupe Indians in Chile this question, "How much of the suffering and poverty of the Machupe is caused directly by the civil government?" I thought Chile would be representative of the problem of state oppression. She said thoughtfully, "About 5%." I was surprised! She said that though there was some problem with the state, the main problems that oppressed the people were liquor and a mentality of adultery. The people literally drink away any money they have, keeping themselves and their posterity in poverty with all its ramifications. It robs them of the initiative and caring that are necessary to advance. Then they drink more to escape it all. She and her husband had been laboring in one village of the Machupe for about five years with little outward result, when one day a man who was the longtime town drunk saw what Jesus had done for him. He repented of his sins and was born again into God's kingdom. Immediately his life began to change. He began to *care*. First he began to care about his wife and his children in great remorse over his past neglect. Soon he gave up alcohol. Soon came some work and some income. Then he began to help his children clean up. He bought them shoes and clothes. He began to fix up his house. He began to honor his wife. Soon she came to Christ. He began to pay off debt. Literally they began to prosper! His neighbors started to wonder what power had transformed his life. He could tell them from personal experience of the love of Jesus and His power to change lives. This was in stark contrast to their impotent tribal gods. Others began to open their hearts to Jesus. All this had nothing to do with the state, but with the heart of an individual being changed by Jesus.

While visiting missionaries in Guatemala City, I came in contact with some of the city's 20,000 street orphans. These missionaries told me that the primary cause of the problem is adultery: a man marries, fathers children, then leaves for another woman. Culturally this is expected by the men, and expected by the women. Children grow up assuming that this is just how life is. The idea that adultery is wrong is something strange. In Brazil there are millions of street orphans. The second cause of the problem is economic. On their own, the mothers cannot feed their children, so they turn them out on the streets. Some roam the streets shining shoes for the day's meal. Others turn to drugs and glue sniffing, and then steal for their meals. The children have no education, love or discipline. In twenty years, what will these millions be doing? They will be totally ungovernable and totally dependent. They will need a strong external government to maintain order.

The answer to these moral and economic problems is the gospel of Jesus Christ. How much pain and bitterness would be removed from any society if adultery were removed, if solid, loving, two-parent families raised the children, and there was abundant economic opportunity?

There is famine in Somalia, but exacerbating the problem is the animosity that the tribes who control the ports have against the tribes inland. There is food on ships in the harbor rotting, but these tribes would just as soon see their fellow countrymen starve to death. The United Nations began a program to guard this relief food and deliver it by force of arms! Foreign armies may perhaps help for a time, but the problem is the <u>hearts</u> of men.

The source of liberty in a society, then, is the Godliness and self-governing character of the people within that society.

CHAPTER III.

THE THREE PHILOSOPHIES OF GOVERNMENT
Healing the nations.

How does God go about bringing a nation from slavery and fear to liberty and peace, from chaos to order, from ignorance to wisdom, from poverty to prosperity?

As the sons of Israel entered the land of promise after their 40-year wandering in the desert, God gave them a stern warning to guide them. It was not political, economic or military in nature, but personal:

> "Only be strong and courageous, to be careful to do according to all the law which Moses My servant commanded you. Do not turn aside from it to the right or the left, so that you may have success wherever you go.
>
> "This book of the law shall not depart from your mouth, but you shall meditate on it day and night, so that you may be careful to do according to all that is written in it, for then you will make your way prosperous, and then you will have success." Josh. 1:7-8

It would do us well to meditate on this injunction. It is the key to healing the nations. Every word is significant. As the people individually followed God closely and obeyed all His commandments, the result would be prosperity and success and His destiny for them would be fulfilled.

It is helpful to ask, "What is a nation?" Exactly what are the tangible entities that comprise a nation? A nation is comprised of individual people, their relationships together and the body of resources on which they dwell. That's all. These relationships include family, educational, business, ecclesiastical and civil relationships, but the only tangible entities are the individual people and the resources. Yet when it is said that a nation is falling apart, we are not talking about the resources, describing an earthquake or a flood. We are speaking of the relationships between people in that nation.

PRINCIPLE: The healing of the nations consists in the healing of individual relationships.

The first relationship to be restored is the individual's relationship with God. Honoring this relationship gives direction and guidance for our thinking and our choices from the perspective of Him who knows — the Creator. Without His input, all we have is a self-centered fixation on feelings and opinions, our own and others'. This describes a condition called "lost." The newspapers chronicle the "lostness" of our society.

Maintaining our relationship with God and getting to know Him more closely, gives the motivation and strength to turn from sin and self-centeredness to love and the highest good. The result of restored relationship with the Creator is, first, an accurate perspective on the dignity and value of the individual. Then in the Bible God gives us the tools to restore and heal personal relationships with others, and the motivation to use them. This describes "salvation" replacing "lostness." Without restored relationship with God, we will only get more lost and pathetic with time, liberal or conservative, secular or religious, right wing or left wing, male or female, black or white. Jesus said that He Himself is the provision for restored relationships with God and others.

The Bible teaches us how then to govern ourselves in every area of life to restore the structures of society to accomplish His good purposes.

There is a sense in the world that democracy should bring about freedom and prosperity and that elections will bring about good civil government and economic success. This is not necessarily the case. While electing a dictator every few years perhaps gives greater liberty than a dictator-for-life, it still does not ensure individual freedom. The only thing that will ultimately bring about good civil government is Biblical, righteous character in the people as a whole. Elections place individuals into office who reflect the character of the people.

It is evident that injustice and bondage exist in society. There are various liberation movements whose avowed intent is to bring liberty to various sectors of society: communism purports to liberate workers, the women's liberation movement to liberate women. But these movements deny the root cause of the tyranny they seek to eliminate, namely individual sin. As such, they cannot actually bring about liberty, but only move society towards chaos and anarchy yielding increased tyranny. We can see this looking at the results of both of these movements.

The communist movement around the world is the self-evident display case of the bondage caused by sin. As the structures have collapsed, chaos not peace has ensued. The new communist man is no better than the old.

Believing that sin and salvation do not exist, the American woman's movement has reacted to societal injustice and personal wounds with rebellion and rejection. Both men and women have swallowed the lie that one's value is defined by one's status, position, toil or task in life. Believing that value is defined by gender, women have come to feel inferior to men, a sense that their "role" is inferior to the "role" of men, and a desperate struggle to prove otherwise has raged. As men have felt threatened, they too have reacted with rejection and harshness. Meanwhile, the devil, the father of lies, is creating havoc.

As women have left the home for the work place, the children have been left to grow on their own, entrusted into the hands of day care workers and televisions. As businesses have begun to assume that families have two breadwinners, they conclude that they don't need to pay as much for each as they did when there was only one. So real wages have actually declined, strangling economic freedom and virtually eliminating a woman's choice to stay at home to raise her family, multiplying the problem. Furthermore, an extreme feminism has developed which rejects men, rejects self for lesbianism, and rejects life for abortion. The end of this is destruction, the consequence of denying the existence of sin. "There is a way which seems right to a man, but its end is the way of death," (Pr. 14:12).

The Bible tells us, however, that men and women are of equal value and that this value is both intrinsic and infinite, not defined by task, gender, position, race, looks, following or any other external thing. We must reject the world's notion of the assumed inequality of people as a lie and stop living our lives in a quest to create value for ourselves. We will never create for ourselves infinite value; God wants us to rest in Him, recognize who He made us to be and love our neighbor as ourself.

VIEW OF SOVEREIGNTY

We saw in the previous chapter that the first aspect of a philosophy of government is the source of government. The second aspect of a philosophy of government (not civil government yet) is our view of sovereignty. This is our view of who or what is in control.

All philosophies and ideologies rest upon one or the other of two ultimate presuppositions. Either 1) the personal, infinite God of the Bible exists, or 2) the personal, infinite God of the Bible does not exist. Both of these presuppositions cannot be true. One of these presuppositions must be true and one must be false; they are mutually irreconcilable. These presuppositions each define worldviews. Each person decides individually which is the most reasonable to believe. He is then morally bound to live as consistently as possible with what he sees as true, and strives to do just that.

Refer to the Sovereignty Grid chart, Fig. 3.4. If we believe that God does not exist, then there are two possible answers to our question, "Who or what has ultimate authority?" Either the state has ultimate authority, or the individual in and of himself has ultimate authority. The Sovereignty Grid helps us categorize the implications of these three views of sovereignty.

SOVEREIGNTY GRID - THE STATE

left extreme	Biblical	right extreme
Presupposition: God does not exist the individual is sovereign anarchy no civil control no gov't	Presupposition: God exists God is sovereign liberty with law gov't by consent internal gov't	Presupposition: God does not exist the state is sovereign tyranny total civil control external gov't

Fig. 3.4 Sovereignty Grid: "Who or what is in control?"

THE STATE IS SOVEREIGN

One of the options for our view of sovereignty is that the state is sovereign - that supreme authority rests in the state. This view is represented on the right side of the sovereignty grid.

In the extreme, what the state decrees is absolute and right by definition and all must obey. In other words the state is God. Here the state decides who should live and who should not, what the individual can and cannot do, what his career will be, how many children he may have, what property he may have, how much of his earnings he may keep, what he may do with his property, what he may think and tell others, where he may travel and what he may teach his children. The state gives rights to life, liberty and property as it wills and takes these rights away as it wills. Since the state is sovereign, anything that expands the power and influence of the state is good and anything that works against the state is bad. The individual is seen as a mere component of the state. The energy and resources of citizens are regarded as belonging to the state and are to be used to aggrandize it.

Employing the educational, media and political elites, the state's job is to control the lives of the people. If it were true that the state is sovereign, then this is what it should actually do. This is tyranny: total civil control.

Finally, if the state is sovereign, then the state should be worshipped. The conclusion that the state is God has been reached in different civilizations at different times in history. Pharaoh in

Egypt believed he was God (Ex. 2:16), Nebuchadnezzar in Babylon (Dan. 3:1-30), Darius in Babylon (Dan. 6:1-28), Herod in Jerusalem (Matt. 2:16), Nero in Rome, etc. — all believed they were ultimate authority and should receive worship.

In the first century there was a big problem for Rome. Caesar believed he was God and demanded the allegiance of the people by their declaration that "Caesar is Lord." But throughout his empire there was a small group called Christians who said "no," to this but said "Jesus is Lord!" This was treason. In every other aspect, these Christians were model citizens and a great asset, paying their taxes, taking care of the poor and preaching and practicing a high standard of personal morality. However, not proclaiming Caesar as lord was punishable by a horrible death by being eaten by lions, burned alive or crucified. Even so, many gave up their lives rather than deny the Lord Jesus, whom they knew and loved.

The view that the state is God was at its height in the Roman Empire during New Testament times.

The Bible indicates the ultimate end of this view to be a single, global tyranny.

THE INDIVIDUAL IS SOVEREIGN

There are individuals who rebel against this control, reasoning that "The state is actually just people like me; what gives them the right to tell me what to do?"

If we believe that God does not exist and the state is not sovereign, then our only alternative is that the individual in and of himself must be sovereign. This view is represented on the left side of the sovereignty grid. In this extreme, each person is autonomous in his own life and chooses for himself what values will be his and what rules of conduct he will abide by. Here it is thought generally, "I can do what I want as long as it doesn't hurt others," but since there is no actual basis for "... as long as it doesn't hurt others, " it comes down to simply, "I can do whatever I want." If it is true that each individual is sovereign, he should actually be able to do anything he wants, hurt others or not.

This is anarchy: no civil control. As we have seen, it is only a transitional phase leading to tyranny. People need and want order and peace, and in times of anarchy look for a strong leader on whom they can depend. A young man from the Caucasus Mountains in Russia told me recently with fist clenched, "My father loved a strong leader who would control the people. We love strong leaders." The brutal dictator Stalin was his father's idol.

In the May 1985 issue of National Geographic there appeared an article on Uganda. It described how, in a civil war in 1979, Idi Amin had been driven out of power. Amin had been an iron-fisted, blood-thirsty dictator for many years. The writer states that since the fall of Amin (six years) "four successive governments have failed to quell the waves of anarchy, murder and chaos that plague Uganda." He said that he was amazed at "how many people tell me that conditions are worse than under Amin. Then murder was systematic, now it is random massacres." The people were wanting to go back to a tyrant strong enough to maintain order. If the people do not govern themselves to do right, a government of external force will arise to fill the vacuum. The *answer* is the gospel of Jesus Christ.

GOD IS SOVEREIGN

The third alternative to the world's system of tyranny vs. anarchy is the view that God is sovereign. This presupposes that God exists and is active in the world today. God's sovereignty means that He has supreme authority over men and nations. It is only in this view that hope exists.

The Bible tells us that God created the heavens and the earth and that He is sovereign. He created us with the ability to govern our lives individually in our relationships with Him and with each other (Matt. 22:36-40). He told us how to do that by giving us laws to which men should conform and the state should conform. This means that government is not derived from the opinions and passions of people, but is to rest on the infinite wisdom of the all-knowing, all-powerful benevolence of the Creator. His statutes take into account everything that we do not know or understand, and are motivated by the desire to secure the highest good. The misery we see in the world is the simple result of man's pride, and rebellion against God's government of wisdom and love.

God has also told us that the purpose of the state is to reward good and punish evil (Rom. 13:3-4). The state has a proper function to provide protection and to secure the 'natural rights' of the individual. Tyranny exists to the degree the state oversteps its proper boundaries.

So to the degree that God's sovereignty is recognized by the people in a society, we have freedom without chaos and order without tyranny because the Law is written on our hearts (Rom. 2:15). The people govern themselves individually under God, according to His Law and ways. Once again we can conclude:

PRINCIPLE: The source of liberty is individual Christian character.

This Christian self-government is how God changes nations and is the alternative to the chaos and oppression of "the kingdoms of this world."

CHAPTER IV.

THE HAND OF GOD IN HISTORY I

Creation through Babel

This chapter begins to summarize the unfolding of the basic principles of Christian self-government through the Bible. The principles are not new but this may be an instructive perspective from which to analyze them. We will view the Bible stories and narrative from the perspective of God's government and see the particulars in the light of God's sovereignty. We will trace the hand of God in the lives of individuals and nations through the Bible. This is a "Big Picture" view of the Scriptures. Later, we will apply our findings to ourselves individually, to our society and to the world. As we understand what God is doing, we can better understand what we should do.

God is a God of purpose. God has a plan for history and is bringing about His plan. God is doing far more in the world today than the devil is doing. This is truly good news!

PRINCIPLE: God's purpose in history is liberty to the individual, internal and external.

God's purpose in the life of the individual Christian is that he be conformed to the image of Christ (Rom. 8:29). God's purpose in the church is to prepare a pure and spotless bride for His Son Jesus, to reign with Him for eternity (Rev. 21:2). But God's purpose in human history is "liberty to the individual" (II Cor. 3:17). As we have seen, God's liberty has two components: internal liberty and external liberty. The first and primary component - internal liberty - comes about as the individual returns to a personal relationship with God through Jesus Christ. He is thus freed from the bondage of sin and guilt. This comes by the grace of God through repentance towards God and faith in the Lord Jesus Christ! This relationship is maintained by a continuing walk of faith and personal righteousness.

Following this internal liberty is external liberty, freedom in the structures of society: family, ecclesiastical, civil and economic. This liberty comes about as the Bible and Christian character are applied to every area of life.

Throughout the Bible, God proclaims and describes Himself as the Lord, the King, the Sovereign One, King of kings, Lord of lords, all authority, the Name above all names and other titles referring to His sovereignty. All these terms speak of government. As Christians, we know that God is sovereign and that men ought to yield to His sovereignty, certainly for their own good and for the good of others but especially for the pleasure of Him who created us. He then suffered, died and rose again for us, so that we could come back into relationship with Him.

The study of the Bible is the study of God's purpose and God's government, of man's response or lack of response to His rule and the ensuing consequences both to God and to man. To study the Bible, then, is to study government and how God's government applies to men both personally in their own lives and affairs and corporately at every level.

THEME I: CREATION God creates man to bless.

In the Bible, chapters 1 through 3 of Genesis are primarily about government: God's authority, the authority He gave men and men's responsibility to obey God's authority.

PRINCIPLE: God is sovereign.

The word "sovereign" means "supreme in authority, possessing supreme dominion" (Webster). God is supreme in authority; He is king over all. In addition, He is supreme in power, love, knowledge and wisdom. In His sovereignty, God created man to be governed by His benevolent rule, and to "have dominion over" or to govern his environment. All this was intended for the great blessing of all (Gen. 1:26).

THE IMAGE OF GOD

God created man distinct from the rest of creation in that man was created in the "image and likeness" of God. Among other things, this refers to man being a personal being as God is. 'Personal' refers to God's attributes of mind, will and emotions. These are attributes which God gave man: a mind with which to think, a will with which to choose and emotions with which to feel. This separates man from the animal kingdom.

Man was created to govern and was given the wonderful ability of free will to make self-originating choices. He was to govern himself under God, choosing according to God's laws and ways. Man's job was also to govern his environment. Along with this ability to choose comes the awesome responsibility to choose the right and reject the wrong. Internal government is voluntarily submitting to the Lordship of Christ, voluntarily doing right. Absolutes do exist.

PRINCIPLE: Man is responsible

We have been given by God the ability to make real choices. We have real input into the world and are to bring only good into it. Though influenced by many things, our choices are not caused by anything external or internal so we ourselves are to blame for our own wrong choices.

In the secular view, men have evolved to their present form by sheer chance interaction of molecules. Society itself is just the aggregate of multiple individuals. There is no choice involved in molecules bouncing around, of course, so men's actions are actually caused, it is said, by heredity, environment and training. The Humanist Manifesto I (1933) states, "Holding an organic view of life, humanists find that the traditional dualism of mind and body must be rejected."[3] The Humanist Manifesto II (1973) continues this view stating, "As far as we know, the total personality is a function of the biological organism transacting in a social and cultural context."[4] If the individual is only a complex chemical reaction, with no spiritual component, then we can look at a simple reaction to understand the secular concept of responsibility.

Suppose I am in a college chemistry lab heating a beaker of water with my Bunsen burner. This is a simple cause-and-effect reaction. Suppose I then address the water with a command, "Get cold!" No matter how forcefully I demand, the water will continue to heat up. The water is being caused to do what it is doing; it does not have freedom and cannot do otherwise. My command is a useless command.

Suppose I then appeal to the water saying, "It is wrong for you to disobey me and not to get cold!" This is absurd, of course. In a cause-and-effect system there is no such concept or notion as right and wrong. Real responsibility does not exist. Suppose I threaten punishment, "If you don't get cold I'll throw you in jail!" or "If you don't get cold I'll send you to hell for eternity!" This is absurd also. In a cause-and-effect system there is no such thing as accountability. This is why it is believed that if homosexual behavior (or any other behavior) can be causally linked to a gene then it cannot be wrong.

PRINCIPLE: That which is caused cannot be free; that which is free cannot be caused.
>   **COROLLARY:** That which is caused is not responsible.
>   **COROLLARY:** That which is caused is not accountable.

So if a person is only a "biological organism transacting in a social and cultural context," then there is no such thing as actual right and wrong, responsibility or accountability. This is the conclusion reached in both Humanist Manifesto documents. Thus we are educating our society away from personal responsibility on every side.

Life doesn't work that way, however. If a drunk driver hits a pedestrian with his car, it is not the bumper of the car that is put in jail, even though it was the bumper that killed the pedestrian. It is not the frame of the car which drove the bumper that is arrested, nor is it the engine which powered the frame that drove the bumper that struck the pedestrian. The individual behind the wheel is held responsible because his actions are not caused but are free and chosen, therefore responsible and accountable.

There are certain aspects of our existence that are cause-and-effect. If I have a headache, I can produce the desired effect of relief by applying an adequate cause such as aspirin. But that is not all that man is. There is a spiritual aspect to man as well as a material one. That is why we can't talk a person out of cancer, nor can we produce a pill that changes rebellion to love, or that saves a person's marriage.

The Bible tells us that we have the ability to choose and are actually responsible, and that we are accountable to eternity for our choices. Our choices are significant. We must choose according to what God sees is the highest good, whether or not we understand, agree, or feel like it, because He created all and knows all. Therefore:

PRINCIPLE: To obey God is intelligence.

THE REBELLION

These chapters of Genesis also include the unfortunate event of Eve's and Adam's yielding to temptation, their refusal to obey God and the grave consequences of that disobedience. Not to obey God is stupidity.

The garden command, "From the tree of the knowledge of good and evil you shall not eat," was the command for self-government under God (Gen. 2:16-17). God said to Adam in effect, "You govern yourself according to My laws and My ways." They were to love God in their hearts and in their actions. God blessed them with every other tree to eat. He told them that the consequence for obedience was life and the consequence for disobedience was death, and they understood (Gen. 3:2-3).

Yet, though they knew the right thing to do, they did it not. This is the definition of sin given in James 4:17: "To him who knows the right thing to do and does it not, to him it is sin." Yielding to temptation, they refused to be governed by God. They chose their own way and rebelled, and began to reap the consequences.

PRINCIPLE: The purpose of Law is protection.

Death means "separation," and the death of which God warned them was immediately evident. They died spiritually at once. The harmony and relationship between man and God was broken as their guilt and resulting fear drove them to hide from God. God's attitude towards them had not changed; He loved them. But their guilt distorted their picture of Him, so they ran. "Your iniquities have caused a separation between you and your God," (Is. 59:2). Man has been running from God ever since.

Social death in their relationship with each other came next as their guilt drove them to hide from each other with clothes, blame each other for their own sin, and reject each other.

After this came physical death. Though they were created to live forever, now the distortion that sin brought affected even their physical existence, dramatically shortening their life span. Eternal death, separation from God and others for eternity, is the ultimate consequence of sin.

PRINCIPLE: There are consequences to every moral choice we make, good consequences (peace and blessing) for right choices and bad consequences (guilt and pain) for wrong choices. Gal. 6:7-8

We can see in Genesis 3:12 that they began to say that God is responsible for the sin in the world, and in verse 13 that Satan is responsible for the sin in the world. And millennia later, men are still saying that. But man alone is responsible for the sin in the world. The wonderful message of the Bible is that if anyone will repent and turn back to God through Jesus Christ, God will forgive him and transform him and restore that relationship once again. Jesus came that we could have life abundant and life eternal (John 10:10, 17:3).

The second source of government is external. Here the individual is governed by external things such as circumstances. After Adam and Eve sinned, God added externally governing forces in the form of circumstances in Gen. 3:14-17. These consisted of pain in bringing forth children, and toil in obtaining food. The Hebrew word for "pain" in verse 16 and for "toil" in verse 17 is the same word: "itstsabon." The connotation is a painful toil in both areas.

This external limitation on both pleasure and free time was intended to slow the progression of evil now that man had brought sin into the world. Who can imagine what we have lost because of sin? This is commonly called "the curse." Strictly speaking, only the serpent and the ground were cursed, not the man or the woman. But circumstances were changed. God's purpose for this change of circumstance was for their good, considering what had taken place.

The next externally governing force imposed by God was His removal of Adam and Eve from the garden, specifically to keep them from eating from the tree of life and living forever in their fallen state and to make possible the provision for salvation (Gen. 3:22). Man was to cultivate the ground that was now cursed (Gen. 3:23-24).

PRINCIPLE: When I refuse to govern myself in an area of my life, authority over my life shifts upward.

Here we see the importance of governing ourselves, and how it affects our freedom. If I do not control myself to do what is right voluntarily, someone else will control me. In this case, authority shifted upwards to God Himself. God implemented circumstances beyond Adam's control to govern him for the highest good now that he had refused to govern himself.

Even with these new external circumstances, the command was still for self-government under God, men were still to govern themselves according to God's ways. In Genesis 4 Cain became jealous and was angry with Abel. But God said, "Sin is crouching at the door... but you must master it." In other words, "You must govern yourself and do what is right." Cain rebelled, however, doing what he felt like rather than what God said, and killed his brother. Once again, God changed the external circumstances: it would now take all Cain had to survive. At the same time, Cain feared vengeance, so God "set a mark" of protection on him saying that no one should take vengeance on him. Again, authority shifted upwards because of sin, and God administered the consequences. Man did not have authority over man at this time.

THE FLOOD

By Genesis 6, we read that internal government had almost completely died out, that mankind had become wicked and violent universally. In fact, "every intent of the thoughts of [men's] hearts was only evil continually. And the Lord was sorry that he had made man on the earth, and he was grieved in his heart," (Gen. 6:5-6).

This is the great love of God for men. Who can conceive of such grief on the level of God's great heart, as He finally decided to bring judgment? Yet Noah loved and obeyed and walked with Him and found favor in His eyes (Gen. 6:8-9). As men had refused to govern themselves under Him, God now brought a drastic externally governing circumstance —- the Flood. This was only after 120 years of warning and pleading by Noah, and striving by the Holy Spirit (Gen.6:3). Evidently no one repented and Noah and his family were brought through the flood on the Ark. God literally started over.

After the Flood, there were many changes. It seems the ground was no longer cursed (Gen. 8:21); the weather was different (8:22); they had a new diet (9:3); the atmosphere was different (9:13). The land masses had changed to be essentially as they are now.

GOD INSTITUTES CIVIL GOVERNMENT

God also for the first time gave men a small amount of authority over men for certain specific purposes. This man-over-man authority is civil government and operates in addition to internal government.

> "And surely I will require your lifeblood, from every beast I will require it. And from man, from every man's brother I will require the life of man.
> "Whoever sheds man's blood
> By man his blood shall be shed,
> For in the image of God
> He made man." Gen. 9:5-6

God's command here is that the life of willful murderers will be taken. The reason stated for this is that the individual is made in the image of God. This has to do with the value of the individual.

PRINCIPLE: The individual is of infinite intrinsic value. All individuals are of equal intrinsic value.

God Himself is of ultimate value. Because man was created in the image of God, he is of infinite value individually. This value is intrinsic, not dependent on gender, race, age, position, wealth, influence, proximity with respect to the womb, health, deformity or any other external thing. This value is infinite. No amount of cows or horses or dollars is equal to the value of an individual human life having been made in the image of God. So if someone takes another's life willfully, he forfeits his own. The purpose of this requirement has to do with public justice.

Who should do this? "Every man's brother" indicates that this is required of the body politic. In order for the body to execute justice, there would have to be some kind of cooperative system set up to ascertain a certainty of guilt to satisfy everyone publicly that justice is being done. This covenant was instituted to end the system of vengeance that reigned before the Flood. The purpose of this requirement was to protect the sanctity of human life made in the image of God. God says here that the life of the individual is sacred and not to be arbitrarily violated.

PRINCIPLE: The purpose of civil government is protection.

Here God gives man a measure of authority over men for the specific purpose of protecting the individual, not controlling him. People are to govern themselves under God; the state is to provide society with protection from those who refuse to do so, controlling the evil.

God says, "I will require..." Doing less constitutes rebellion. The case has been argued against capital punishment that it does not deter criminals or crime and therefore should not be applied. The purpose of this requirement, however, is not deterrence but public justice.

While living in Holland in 1975, I noted that at the time the penalty for murder was two years in prison. The concept of the sanctity or value of human life that this produces is very low indeed. This is rebellion against God. Fifteen years later, some 25% of deaths in the Netherlands were from euthanasia, voluntary and involuntary.

Doing more than the commandment requires constitutes rebellion also, however. In another nation individuals are tortured to death in the public square for even small crimes. The purpose of this barbarity is deterrence, not justice. In this case also the sanctity of human life is eroded. This, too, is rebellion against God.

As stated earlier, there is a relationship between the internal and the external government in a society:

PRINCIPLE: The amount of liberty in a society is defined by and dependent upon the character of the people within that society.

God saw that this balancing combination of internal character and external civil government would be enough to control evil until His purposes were accomplished. He set the rainbow in the sky as the sign of His covenant never to destroy the world again with a flood (Gen. 9:11).

THE TOWER OF BABEL

After the Flood, God once again told the people to multiply and fill the earth (Gen. 9:1). Instead, they gathered together to build a city and a tower to the stars in order to "make a name for themselves" (Gen. 11:4). This became the first kingdom in the Bible and was set up under Nimrod, "a mighty hunter before the Lord" (Gen. 10:10). Nimrod ruled the people as they submitted to him in dependence. This is the first time the word 'kingdom' is used in the Bible. A kingdom arises from a people dependent on man instead of God, and a strong ruler willing to receive their adulation, and control them. It is interesting to note that the word rendered 'before' also connotes 'against' indicating that this kingdom arose out of rebellion against God.

This refusal to obey God resulted in another externally governing circumstance: God confused their language. The people had one language at this time, the language given by God in the beginning. As they had turned to rebellion, their language afforded them virtually limitless power to work together devising evil (Gen. 11:6). God saw that confusing their language would diffuse this rebellion.

Rebellion can only unify around a project, so when the project was abruptly halted by their inability to understand one another, their rebellion turned them against each other. Rebellion does not make the foundation of a tolerable society, so they finally decided to pick up and leave. In this way "the Lord scattered them abroad over the face of the whole earth," (Gen. 11:9).

GOVERNMENTAL PROVIDENCE

It is important to mention that while our emphasis here is on the choices of individuals, we can also see many places in the Bible that speak of special and unusual situations where God Himself acts into events to cause the actions of individuals under what we can call a "Governmental Providence" to bring about His desired ends. This does not have to do with the individual's personal salvation or character, but with other aspects of God's responsibilities such as the rulership of the nations, the first and second coming of Christ and fulfillment of prophesy. Under such a case, we can see that the individual's responsibility and accountability would be suspended for that particular action only. For all of his own choices, the individual remains accountable. We see both of these aspects interwoven throughout the Bible.

CHAPTER V.

THE HAND OF GOD IN HISTORY II

Abraham through Malachi

THEME II: REDEMPTION - God prepares a people for Godly self-government and liberty.

In Genesis 12, God begins His plan of redemption by calling Abraham from his home in Ur of the Chaldees to leave his country, his relatives and his father's house, to trust Him and go to the place that He would show him. "So Abraham went forth" in faith (Gen 12:1-4).

Abraham then begot Isaac, Isaac begot Jacob and Esau, and Jacob had 12 sons, one of whom, Joseph, was sold by his brothers into slavery in Egypt. Eventually, God caused Joseph to become the effective head of Egypt under Pharaoh. Joseph later brought his whole family (70 persons in all) to Egypt to survive the Canaan famine. In four centuries that family grew into a great nation within Egypt.

A KINGDOM OF PRIESTS

Over time, as the sons of Israel grew in number, "a new king arose over Egypt who did not know Joseph" (Ex. 1:8). This new king feared the sons of Israel and began to afflict them and try to kill them off. God then raised up Moses, first training him in Pharaoh's court and then training him out in the desert for the job He had for him — to lead the sons of Israel and bring them back into the land of Canaan.

God used Moses to bring the Israelites out of Egypt and into the desert with great signs and miracles. In the wilderness, God brought them up to Mount Sinai. There He said to them:

> "If you will indeed obey My voice and keep My covenant, then you shall be My own possession among all the peoples, for all the earth is Mine; and you shall be to Me a kingdom of priests and a holy nation." Ex. 19:5-6

And the people agreed.

A kingdom of priests is an arrangement in which God is King and each individual, being a priest, has personal access to God the King. Out in the wilderness, they were free and had no Pharaoh ruling over them. They were looking up to God. This is represented in Fig. 5.1.

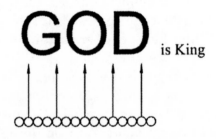

Fig. 5.1 Kingdom Of Priests

God appointed leadership for them in the wilderness to help them to know and follow Him. In Fig. 5.2, Moses is their leader. The leader is represented below the people to indicate his character of humility and servanthood.

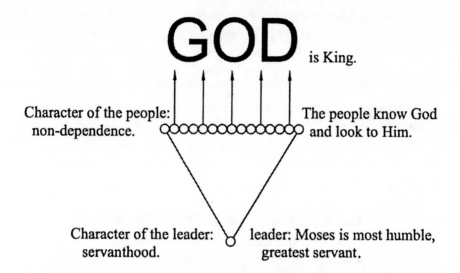

Fig. 5.2 Israel In The Wilderness.

God gives authority to men on the basis of servanthood (Matt. 20:25-28). So in the illustration, while the leader's position is below the individual, it represents the position of true authority. Moses' ministry was to help the people to know God, obey God (govern themselves under Him) and serve God. Moses was to serve God and the people in this way.

Then God gave the people the Ten Commandments (Ex. 20). The command once again was for individual Godly self-government. They were to govern themselves according to God's dictates. They were now blessed to know exactly how to do that! God gave the Ten Commandments so the people would know what is right and wrong and to protect them from the consequences of evil. These are not arbitrary directions from above, but expressions of how we were created. They are a description of reality. In order for the creation to work the way it was intended to work, we must heed them.

If I own a car and the designer says to put five quarts of oil in it, I had better do it or destruction will ensue. If I don't know I am to do this, destruction will still ensue. The requirement is not arbitrary, but describes reality and there's no way to get around it. To obey the Ten Commandments is to live intelligently and naturally, as God created us.

There are four categories of laws that God gave for the sons of Israel. First was the moral law, the Ten Commandments. These are moral absolutes. They have always been and will always be in every place the moral code. They will be the moral code in heaven. Jesus expanded on the letter of the law to include the spirit of these laws in the Sermon on the Mount and elsewhere (Matt. 5-7). Not only is murder wrong, but being angry with your brother is wrong.

As Moses recounted these ten absolutes to the people in Deuteronomy 5, God mades a distinction between these laws and all the other ordinances:

> "These words the Lord spoke to all your assembly at the mountain from the midst of the fire, the cloud, and the thick gloom, with a great voice, and He added no more. And He wrote them on two tablets of stone and gave them to me." Deut. 5:22

This indicates that the Ten Commandments are in a different class from the others in that "He added no more." Nine verses later God tells Moses:

> "But as for you, stand here by Me, that I may speak to you all the commandments and the statutes and the judgements which you shall teach them, that they may observe them in the land which I give them to possess." Deut. 5:31

These commandments were of three basic categories: dietary laws, civil laws and ceremonial laws. These were God's commands to the sons of Israel, but were not absolute in the sense of the moral law, the Ten Commandments. We know that the ceremonial laws were eliminated when Jesus became the once-for-all sacrifice for our sins. The dietary laws were altered in Acts 10:10-16. The purpose of Law is protection.

EGYPTIAN SLAVERY

Back in Egypt, the Israelites had been enslaved. This is represented in Fig. 5.3:

In Egypt, the individual was the servant of the state and the state's job was to rule and control his life. The people looked to Pharaoh. Pharaoh told them what their vocation was, whether they could use straw in their bricks, whether they could serve God, and even whether their children could live and what gender their children must be. In other words, "The state is God." Here the value of the individual is not intrinsic but is defined by his contribution to the state.

This is the pagan view of man and the state (pagan meaning not recognizing God's authority). The Pharaoh controlled every aspect of their lives. They served him and he fed them. In the diagram, the ruler is represented above the people, signifying an authority of external force and fear.

Mentality of the ruler: external control.

ruler: Pharoah is king.

Character of the people: dependence.

The people don't know God, look to ruler.

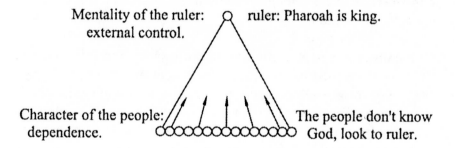

Fig. 5.3 Egypt - Pagan Dictatorship

Here we see the difference between a ruler and a leader. In Fig. 5.2 the individual is the servant of God and the leadership structure is the servant of the individual providing *protection*. In Fig. 5.3 the individual is the servant of the state, and the ruler *controls* and directs the individual's life.

PRINCIPLE: The Christian view of man and the state is that

God is sovereign, the individual is the servant of God, and the state is the servant of the individual. The Pagan view of man and the state is that the State is sovereign and the individual is the servant of the State.

Out in the wilderness, God now invited (commanded) the people of Israel to obey Him and be a kingdom of priests to Him. They were now a nation without a human king. God was now their king. Moses was their leader.

As they made their way across the desert, however, their inner character of dependence on the state and lack of knowledge of God was manifested at ten crisis points. They wanted to go back to Egypt for those "free" leeks and onions (Num. 11:4-6). To them, life was easier back in Egypt because they didn't have to think, choose, be creative, obey God or trust God. Now they had to trust God for their provision, their direction and their future. The generation that left Egypt couldn't handle the personal responsibility and wanted to go back to the "easier" life in Egyptian slavery.

PRINCIPLE: Bondage is voluntary. Freedom takes Godly character to maintain.

Finally, at the edge of the land of promise, they rebelled against Moses and decided to appoint a new leader and return to Egypt (Num. 14). Moses interceded for them in prayer and God made a new decision. For the next 40 years they would learn and develop the freedom character of dependence on God and teach it to their children. The generation that thus entered Canaan 40 years later was cleansed of the slavery character of dependence on the state. God had to go around the generation that would not believe Him, but he loved the sons of Israel too much to let them go back to slavery.

THE PROMISED LAND

The next generation entered Canaan full of faith. God reminded them to obey all of His law, saying that as a nation they are first built internally, then externally. First comes character, then prosperity and success as a nation:

"This book of the law shall not depart from your mouth, but you shall meditate on it day and night, so that you may be careful to do according to all that is written in it; for then you will make your way prosperous, and then you will have success." Josh. 1:8

PRINCIPLE: Intimacy with God is primary. Civil liberty and success is consequential.

The command was again for individual Godly self-government: to be careful to obey all of God's law. God was their King and they were individually to obey His laws and ways. They were told to "meditate day and night" on His Law. God appointed leaders for them, judges and prophets to serve them and help them to know and serve God. They were not intended to have a human king. God was their king. As long as they followed God, they were free.

Through Joshua and Judges, whenever the Israelites would fall away from God, and do what was evil in His sight, their freedom turned into license and anarchy. Their neighbors would perhaps look in and say something like, "They're weak and in disarray. Now is our chance!" They recognized that if the Israelites wouldn't control themselves morally, neither would they sacrifice and organize to rebuff an invasion. And the Lord would allow the sons of Israel to be defeated by their enemies. This is a violent warning to us.

When the sons of Israel would turn back to God and cry out to Him in repentance, He would raise up a leader to deliver them again.

The Israelites had been at their peak in character when they crossed the Jordan. They trusted God and obeyed Him, and God did mighty miracles to plant them in the Land of Promise. Over the years (generations), however, their hearts began to turn from Him and their relationship with Him became more an external religion. His reality as their king began to fade, and they began to feel, "We have no king!" Unless one is born again, he cannot see the kingdom of God (John 3:3).

This shift in character can be seen as early as Judges 8 when Gideon delivered Israel from the Midianites. After he was used by God to deliver them, the people saw Gideon as a mighty man and approached him saying, "Rule over us... for you have delivered us from the hand of Midian," (Judg. 8:22). They were growing dependent in character and they wanted a mighty king, a ruler; slavery is voluntary. But Gideon said to them, "I will not rule over you... the Lord shall rule over you." After all that God had done to call him to the task and accomplish it, Gideon knew Who had delivered them.

As Israel's character continued to decline internally, horrendous things were happening in Israel. God had faded away in their hearts as their king, and they had no human king either. The book of Judges is the candid chronicle of this anarchy as liberty is turned to unrestrained license. Thus the last words of the book of Judges are, "In those days there was no king in Israel; everyone did what was right in his own eyes," (Judg. 21:25). Unfortunately, instead of repenting of the license, they chose external restraint.

THEME III: THE KINGDOM OF ISRAEL - The people want an earthly king and slavery.

During this time, Samuel was born and grew up. The people recognized him as their prophet, and he served them and helped them follow the Lord. In I Samuel 7, the Philistines were about to wage war with the Israelites. But at Samuel's decree, the Israelites returned to the Lord, removed the false gods of Baal and the Ashteroth, and "served the Lord alone" (v4). They gathered at Mizpah and repented before the Lord. As Samuel cried out to the Lord on their behalf, the Philistines drew up to attack them. But the Lord "thundered with a great voice on that day" so that they were confused and routed before Israel.

However, despite God's miraculous deliverance, the people became less and less dependent on Him and more dependent on Samuel, as the Lord continued to fade in their hearts. They were in effect looking to Samuel and his sons as their king. In their hearts, the triangle in Fig. 5.2 was inverting. When Samuel grew old, they saw trouble coming: Samuel would soon die and his sons were not worthy to rule.

ISRAEL DEMANDS A KING

Then in I Samuel 8, "all the elders of Israel" came to Samuel and said, "Appoint us a king to judge us like all the nations." A disheartened Samuel saw that this was evil and sought the Lord. The Lord said to Samuel, "Listen to the voice of the people in regard to all that they say to you, for they have not rejected you, but they have rejected Me from being king over them." Their character and relationship with God had declined until they did not see God as their king any more and perceived the cause of their vulnerability to surrounding nations as the lack of a king "like all the nations." But this was not God's plan for them, and He tells Samuel to warn them of the slavery that would come upon them if they had a king (I Sam. 8:10-18). God adds to His warning:

> "Then you will cry out in that day because of your king whom you have chosen for yourselves, but the Lord will not answer you in that day. I Sam. 8:18

The reason God would not answer in that day was not because He was vindictive and their suffering would serve them right, but because their character was at the breaking point right then between dependence on God and dependence on man. That moment was the time to return in their hearts to God. If they had a king they would grow more and more dependent in character and less and less able to handle liberty. They could barely handle it now! It would grow increasingly difficult for God to reverse what they were now demanding.

"No, but there shall be a king over us, that we may be like all the nations, that our king may judge us and go out before us and fight our battles," they said (v19). They nevertheless wanted a human king to depend upon rather than God. This took place in 1120 B.C.

So God said, "Appoint them a king." They exchanged the kingdom of God for a kingdom of man, the internal rule of God for the external rule of man. Thus slavery is voluntary. As character weakens, the hand of the state is strengthened.

Saul was chosen by God and anointed king by Samuel. Samuel

admonished the people saying,

> "If you will fear the Lord and serve Him, and listen to His voice and not rebel against the command of the Lord, then both you and also the king who reigns over you will follow the Lord your God."
>
> "And if you will not listen to the voice of the Lord, but rebel against the command of the Lord, then the hand of the Lord will be against you as it was against your fathers." I Sam. 12:14-15

The sons of Israel are to continue to look to God and govern themselves under Him. If they do, the state will release liberty. The KJV says, "It will be well." But if they do not look to God, increasing in dependence on Him, their dependence on man will grow and the state will enslave them as had been the situation with their fathers in Egypt.

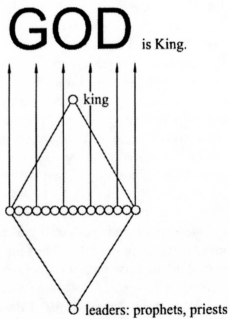

Fig. 5.4 The Kingdom Of Israel

Even though they now had a king, their external liberty would still be defined by their character. The situation was now as in Fig. 5.4.

SAUL, DAVID, SOLOMON

We will assume that Saul was the best man God could find to be king. Over time, however, power corrupted him. Imagine the strength of character necessary to resist corruption with a whole nation bowing down to you and depending on you. It is said that absolute power corrupts absolutely. Over time, Saul began to use state power for personal ends. He became jealous of David's popularity. He wanted his own son to be king, rather than David whom God had anointed, so he spent much of his life hunting David, and finally died an insane, wicked man.

When Saul died, David became king, and though he was "a man after God's heart," he also abused state power and committed adultery and murder. When confronted, David repented (II Sam. 12:13). Saul had been confronted but did not repent, being sorry for what he had done only because of the favor his sin had lost him (I Sam. 15:24-25).

After David, Solomon became king.

Through this time, the kingdom of Israel grew externally in size, in power, and in national identity. It was the golden age of Israel. Solomon built the Temple, making Jerusalem both the civil and the ecclesiastical center of the nation. The kingdom of Israel and the worship of Yahweh became synonymous, a state religion.

The reigns of David and Solomon and all their grandeur and splendor were perceived as the fulfillment of God's destiny for the sons of Abraham—-God's chosen people. Yet internally the people were sliding further and further away from God. This must be a lesson for our nation.

Solomon began well but over 40 years turned from God, though God had appeared to him twice. Solomon sinned by marrying many foreign wives and began to introduce their pagan religions in Israel (I Kin. 11). The people were in agreement. So while externally Israel was booming, internally the people were growing more and more pagan, dependent, chaotic and unrighteous.

JUDGMENT COMES UPON ISRAEL

Finally, after only three kings, judgment came from God. Upon Solomon's death, the kingdom of Israel was divided into two kingdoms in approximately 975 B.C. The Northern Kingdom, Israel, consisted of ten tribes and was ruled in Samaria by Jeroboam, Solomon's servant. The Southern Kingdom, Judah, consisted of Judah and Benjamin and was ruled in Jerusalem by Rehoboam, Solomon's son. God's purpose in this judgment was to split the nation to preserve a remnant that would be faithful to Him. Out of this remnant God would bring forth a Savior.

PRINCIPLE: Personal unrighteousness brings national disintegration.

The Northern Kingdom, Israel, continued to decline in character (internally) as the people strayed from God. Isaiah prophesied their destruction. In the midst of the destruction, he prophesied of a coming Messiah:

> "For a child will be born to us, a son will be given
> to us;
> And the government will rest on His shoulders;
> And His name shall be called Wonderful Counselor,
> Mighty God, Eternal Father,
> Prince of Peace.
> There will be no end to the increase of His
> government or of peace." Is. 9:6

Isaiah says here that the coming child would have a government placed upon His shoulders, that this government would begin to increase, and that there would be no end to its increase or of the resulting peace. Peace is the consequence of Jesus governing.

Israel declined externally also, until judgment came in 722 B.C. Assyria besieged Samaria, and Israel's ten tribes were carried off captive, never to return.

The Southern Kingdom, Judah, also continued to decline in character. Jeremiah prophesied concerning their destruction and 70-year exile until Nebuchadnezzar besieged Jerusalem and deported the people to Babylon in 588 B.C. Daniel was among the exiles and during this time he, too, prophesied of the coming Messiah:

> "And behold, with the clouds of heaven
> One like a Son of Man was coming
> And He came up to the Ancient of Days
> And was presented before Him.
> And to Him was given dominion,
> Glory and a kingdom,
> That all the peoples, nations, and men of every
>   tongue
> Might serve Him.
> His dominion is an everlasting dominion
> Which will not pass away;
> And His kingdom is one which will not be
>   destroyed." Dan. 7:14-15

Daniel prophesied that the kingdom of the Messiah would be everlasting and His dominion forever.

The Jews were in Babylon 70 years; then God brought back a remnant under the leadership of Nehemiah and Ezra to rebuild the Temple and the walls and the city of Jerusalem. The minor prophets encouraged them in this task and in personal righteousness. The last prophet was Malachi, approximately 430 B.C.

Judah grew, but character continued to decline. Judgment came again in 63 B.C. when Jerusalem fell to the Roman general Pompey, and Judea came under the control of Rome.

CHAPTER VI.

THE HAND OF GOD IN HISTORY III

Matthew through Revelation

THEME IV: THE KINGDOM OF GOD - God's new covenant: an internal kingdom.

JESUS THE MESSIAH

"Now in the sixth month, the angel Gabriel was sent from God to a city in Galilee, called Nazareth, to a virgin..." the story is told, to announce to her that she would give birth to the Messiah, the only begotten Son of God, whose kingdom will have no end (Luke 1:26-33). Mary's amazement can hardly be imagined.

Many supernatural signs attended His birth, confirming the identity of the child. At Gabriel's direction to Mary's betrothed, Joseph, he called His name Jesus, in Hebrew Jeshua meaning salvation, for "it is He who will save His people from their sins" (Matt. 1:20-21). This was the Messiah's job. Gabriel did not say that He would save His people from their political situation, from the Romans, but rather from their sins.

When Jesus began to teach, Jerusalem was in great political foment. The Jews were chafing under Roman rule, and the Romans were attempting to maintain civil order. The Jews were waiting for a Messiah whom they thought would be a triumphant king. This Messiah King would supposedly be raised up by God to re-establish David's glorious kingdom, returning the Jews to civil control and displacing the Roman rule. The Jews of the day saw themselves as the people of God chosen for this destiny. They perceived the kingdom of God as an external political kingdom of military might and splendor. Rumors circulating from years before suggested that this Messiah was already somewhere among them.

But Jesus had come to set up a new kingdom in the hearts of men, an internal kingdom that would eventually topple the kingdoms of this world (Rev. 11:15). In Christ's death on the cross for our sins, genuine salvation from guilt and sin is made possible for the individual. An intimate personal relationship with God became once and for all available to all who will turn from their sins and come to the Lord Jesus in faith and obedience. In Christ, we can actually know God personally.

With the advent of this new personal relationship with God, the potential strength of internal government becomes vastly increased. In addition to having the Law, the Ten Commandments, to conform to, now "the love of Christ controls us" (II Cor. 5:14). In Jesus' teaching, we understand not just the letter of God's Law but the spirit of the Law, which is love and the highest good. We learn that not only is murder wrong, but hating our brother is wrong. Not only is adultery wrong, but entertaining lustful thoughts is wrong. In Jesus' death on the cross for us, the door is flung open to a love relationship with the Lawgiver, and we are released from our bondage to sin and guilt. In His resurrection, we have available power to govern our lives in righteousness as we submit to Jesus as our king. Sin ceases to have dominion over us. With Pentecost, we have a new relationship with the God the Holy Spirit for holiness and strength of character, and for being His witnesses to the ends of the earth (Acts 1:8).

Jesus taught the people the values of the kingdom of God. His sermon on the mount was a summary of these values. It was a vivid contrast to the values of the kingdoms of men.

On an outreach to the Balkan nation Kosovo shortly after the 1999 war, I saw firsthand how radical Jesus' teaching was. Simplified, the war was about stopping the ethnic cleansing by the Serbs against the Kosvar Albanians. At this time, however, as the Albanian refugees returned home, they were committing similar plunders against the Serbs. The rule of conduct in that area has been one of vengeance for centuries, not only Serbs and Albanians against each other, but Serb against Serb and Albanian against

Albanian, not unlike many ethnic conflicts in the world.

In response to this, the United Nations was occupying the land, and their peacekeeping troops were everywhere to keep order, basically keeping the Serbs and the Albanians from killing each other. It struck me that every person I met was telling me within minutes what he had suffered at the hands of the opposition. The things they had suffered were truly unbelievable and their experiences left me literally speechless. I had *nothing* to offer.

One night I was particularly vexed, and asking the Lord, "What can I say to these people in their chaos and suffering? What would You say?"

Immediately the Lord showed me that the world into which He came 2000 years ago was very similar in these respects to Kosovo now, only much worse. There was an occupying Roman army keeping order, only that army was not friendly at all. There were ethnic, religious and political factions vying for control. The Romans were very corrupt, even bloodthirsty. The Jews were targets. Atrocities were everywhere. It was even worse than Kosovo today.

Into this cacophony came Jesus, and what He said was, "Repent, for the kingdom of heaven is at hand." The Gospels use the 'kingdom of heaven' and the 'kingdom of God' interchangeably. Try to imagine Jesus on the street corner or in a park teaching and proclaiming kingdom values to the various peoples of Kosovo (please excuse some paraphrase).

"Repent, for the kingdom of heaven is at hand!"

"Blessed are the meek, for they shall inherit the earth." God is opposed to the proud.

"Blessed are those who hunger and thirst after righteousness, for they shall be satisfied." This is how you were created to live.

"Blessed are the merciful, for they shall receive mercy." "Do unto others as you would have them do unto you."

"Blessed are the pure in heart for they shall see God." The impure in heart will <u>not</u> see God.

"Blessed are those who make peace; they shall be called the sons of God." "Be at peace with all men."

"You are the light of the world. Let your light so shine among men that they see your good works and glorify your father in Heaven."

"Whoever keeps God's laws and teaches them, he will be great in the kingdom of heaven." "Unless your righteousness surpasses that of the Scribes and Pharisees [and Bishops and Mullahs] you shall not enter the kingdom of God."

"You have heard it said 'You shall not murder.' But I say unto you whoever is angry with his brother is guilty unto Hell!" "Therefore if you remember that your brother has something against you, go immediately, first be reconciled to your brother, then return and present your offering."

"You have heard it said 'You shall not commit adultery.' But I say to you if you look upon a woman to lust after her, you are guilty of adultery in your heart." "It is better to pluck out your eye than to go to hell because of it."

"You have heard it said, 'Fulfill your vows.' But I say to you let your yes be yes and your no be no." God desires integrity.

"You have heard it said, 'an eye for an eye and a tooth for a tooth.' But I say to you whoever slaps you on your right cheek, turn the other also.

Whoever sues you for your coat, give him your shirt also. Whoever forces you to go one mile, go with him another."

"Give to him who asks you. Lend to him who is in need. Love your neighbor. Love your enemy also. Pray for him; God works in his life also. If you love only your friend, so what. Everyone does that."

"You are to be perfect, as your heavenly father is perfect."

"Don't be religious to be seen of men. God sees your secret acts, and rewards you."

"Don't let your prayers be meaningless repetition." Anyone can do that. Talk to God. Listen to Him. He desires a relationship with you.

"Pray for God's kingdom to come, and for people to do <u>His</u> will. Trust God for your provision each day; don't even be anxious about it."

"Receive God's forgiveness for your sins. Forgive <u>all</u> who have sinned against you. Otherwise He will not forgive you."

"Do not fast to be seen of men. God who sees in secret will repay."

"Do not lay up treasures on earth. They will not last. Lay up treasures in heaven. They are forever. You cannot serve both God and money."

"Don't be anxious for tomorrow. Seek first His kingdom and His righteousness, and all these things will be added to you."

"Don't pass judgment on another, or you will be judged."

"Enter the kingdom of God by the narrow gate" of repentance.

"Beware of false prophets. You will know them by the fruit of their lives."

"The kingdom of God is within you." Obedience to God the king is primary. God is of ultimate value in the universe.

"Love your neighbor as yourself." You are of value equal to every other person; that value is infinite. You are to live that way concerning every person.

"Not everyone who says to me 'Lord, Lord' will enter the kingdom of heaven, but he who does the will of the Father. Many will suppose they are accepted by virtue of being religious, but I never knew them. They will not enter."

"Be content."

Those who loved the Lord received His words and turned to God in repentance. Many were confused by His message, however, not understanding a connection between repentance and the expected coming external earthly kingdom. At one point after Jesus had miraculously fed five thousand people starting with only five barley loaves and two fish (John 6), the gathering, realizing a man of unusual abilities was among them, reasoned, "This is truly the Prophet who is to come into the world!" Their intention became to "take Him by force to make Him king" (John 6:15). Jesus, however, would have no part of this and "went His way."

Jesus' inner circle of twelve disciples also had the false expectation of an external kingdom. At one point, the mother of disciples James and John, came to Jesus with her sons, requesting that "When You come in Your kingdom these two sons of mine may sit, one on Your right and one on Your left" (Matt. 20:20-28). They were asking for the two chief-deputy positions of an external kingdom. But Jesus' kingdom is internal. Jesus answered the sons, "You do not know what you are asking for. Are you able to drink the cup that I am about to drink?" They said to him, "We are able." James and John didn't know that their anticipated king was about to be crucified. Jesus told them, "My cup you shall drink, but to sit on My right and on My left is not mine to give, but it is for those for whom it has been prepared by My Father." The Father, then, prepares the individual for authority and releases him or her into it.

Upon learning of the promotional ambitions of James and John the other ten disciples "became indignant," basically because they didn't want to be left out of power in this new kingdom. Aware of this rift in the group, Jesus called them to Himself and explained that God's kingdom is different from men's kingdoms. He said,

"You know that the rulers of the Gentiles lord it over them... It is not so among you, but whoever wishes to become great among you shall be your servant, and whoever wishes to be first among you shall be your slave; just as the Son of Man did not come to be served, but to serve, and to give His life a ransom for many." Matt. 20:28

In demonstration of this humility, Jesus would eventually wash the feet of those disciples. In this manner Christ demonstrated that the qualification for authority is a character of servanthood, the greatest authority being granted by God to the greatest servant.

PRINCIPLE: Authority is based on servanthood.

JESUS' DEATH AND RESURRECTION

It is well known that Jesus was betrayed by the disciple Judas to the Jewish officials (John 18:1-6). Jesus had said, publicly, that He was the Son of God (Matt. 26:62-66). Those officials brought against Jesus the very serious charge of blasphemy. They turned Him over to the Roman government where He was interrogated by Pontius Pilate, the Roman Governor of Judea.

Pilate asked Jesus bluntly, "You are the king of the Jews?" (John 18:33-38) Jesus answered, "Are you saying this on your own initiative, or did others tell you about me?" Jesus doesn't say "yes" or "no." He, in fact, is their king, but not in the manner the Roman Governor perceives "kingship." Jesus is not in competition with Pilate or Herod (the king of Judea) or even Caesar in Rome. The kingdom of God is not an earthly kingdom. Therefore, Jesus speaks to Pilate of this unearthly concept, "My kingdom is not of this realm." "So, you are a king?" asks Pilate. Jesus replied, "You say correctly that I am a king, for this I have been born, for this I have come into the world" (John 18:37).

The Jewish officials, sensing that Pilate needed convincing, cried out to him, "If you release this man, you are no friend of Caesar; everyone who makes himself out to be a king opposes Caesar" (John 19:12). They missed the point that Jesus' kingdom is internal. The chief priests then declared, "We have no king but Caesar!" (John 19:15). They effectively renounced God as their king in saying this. Jesus said to them, "Your desolation is at hand" (Luke 21:20). Pilate eventually succumbed to the pressure of the chief priests and had Jesus crucified. The third day after Jesus was crucified, He rose again from the dead, verifying His claim of deity.

Even after the resurrection, the disciples of Christ were still expecting an external kingdom. It is recorded in Acts 1:6-8 that they asked yet again, "Lord, is it at this time You are restoring the kingdom to Israel?" Jesus said, "It is not for you to know the times or the epochs which the Father has fixed by His own authority; but you shall receive power when the Holy Spirit has come upon you, and you shall be My witnesses both in Jerusalem, Judea, and Samaria and even to the remotest part of the earth" (Acts 1:6-8). This must have been a puzzling statement to the disciples, who evidently were thinking, "He rose from the dead! This must be it!" Jesus answers neither "yes" nor "no" because He is constructing something new.

Though Jesus' kingdom was the smallest of kingdoms, "like a mustard seed" (Matt. 13:31), He had been given ultimate "authority both in heaven and on earth" (Matt. 28:18). The "ruler of this world" had been "cast out" (John 12:31). God had "raised [Jesus] from the dead and seated Him at His right hand in the heavenlies, far above all rule and authority and power and dominion and every name that is named, not only in this age but also in the one to come" (Eph. 1:21; also Col. 2:10; I Pet. 3:22; Phil. 2:5-11). This was the manifestation of the wisdom of God, "which none of the rulers of this age has understood; for if they had understood it, they would not have crucified the Lord of glory" (I Cor. 2:7-8).

Jesus' kingdom is an internal kingdom. He had metaphorically compared it to leaven, "which a woman took and hid in three pecks of meal, until all was leavened" (Matt. 13:33). This internal kingdom grows quietly, but surely, until it fills the whole earth — every tongue, tribe and nation. The curious facet of this kingdom however is that "unless you are born again, you cannot see the kingdom of God" (John 3:3). Just as the disciples of Jesus, the Jewish leaders and the Roman authorities missed the point, individuals today do not understand the concept of an internal kingdom ruled by God unless they are "born again" into it. Jesus reigns in the hearts of individuals. His entire focus was on character, which would eventually cause entire social structures to change. He barely mentioned the political or ecclesiastical structures, but spoke to individuals of their sin.

God's new program was about to begin!

THEME V: THE EARLY CHURCH - "Of the increase of His government and peace there will be no end." Is. 9:6

PENTECOST

Jesus' kingdom was granted to Him at the resurrection, but a few weeks later, the expansion of this new kingdom began with an immense explosion. The scene developed as many devout Jews from all over the Mediterranean world were visiting Jerusalem for the celebration of Pentecost. The city was filled with religious pilgrims when no less than one hundred and twenty followers of Jesus were unexpectedly "filled with the Holy Spirit" in an upstairs room where they were gathered to pray (Acts 2). They poured out of the upper room "drunk with joy" speaking the praises of God in the various tongues of the foreign visitors, who wondered how the local Jews knew their languages. As the good news of Jesus' incarnation, death and resurrection was explained to the curious visitors, they became aware of the nearness of the new kingdom and, as the event is recorded, "were pierced to the heart" (Acts 2:37). That day, **three thousand** repented and were added to Jesus' kingdom from "every nation under heaven" (Acts 2:5,41).

As all the new converts learned, worshipped and ate together, and began to care about each other with joy, more people around them were converted. The chronicle states in Acts 2:47, "And the Lord was adding to their number day by day those who were being saved."

As the Pentecost pilgrims returned home to the various lands from which they had come, they brought the gospel with them. Each individual from the Pentecost conversion knew, loved and ministered to God. They each received from Him and served Him, and enthusiastically loved their neighbors. In this manner, the letter *and* spirit of the Law was now written on their hearts. As these believers grew in Christ, they became His "witnesses to the ends of the earth" (Acts 1:8). They forgot about "restoring the kingdom to Israel." They understood, at last, that God was doing something new.

GENEROSITY

It is interesting to note that many of these visitors to Jerusalem at the time of Pentecost had come from nations far away, not intending to remain long and not bringing extra provision. After the outpouring of the Holy Spirit, however, they stayed on to receive the Apostles' teaching and gain understanding as to what had happened to them, and what it would mean in their lives. In their excitement they began to run out of provisions, so the local believers began to supply their needs in a great outpouring of generosity.

> "And everyone kept feeling a great sense of awe," the story continues "and many wonders and signs were taking place through the Apostles. And all those who had believed were together, and had all things in common; and they began selling their property and possessions, and were sharing them with all as anyone might have need." Acts 2:43-45, reiterated in 4:32-35

Some use these verses to justify an idea of collectivism as God's New Testament economic system. But this was not a newly legislated communal property system, but a spontaneous and voluntary outpouring of love and generosity in the Holy Spirit by local believers to help their new brethren from far-off lands. It was marked by great joy.

THE END OF THE AGE

Jesus, during his public ministry, had wept over the city Jerusalem saying, "If you had known this day the things which make for peace" (Luke 19:41-42). His pleading with the people to repent and turn back to the kingdom of God had been met with a violent rejection that ultimately resulted in His crucifixion — the Savior, the Son of God.

Personal character in Judea continued to decline until, in 70 AD, Judea was utterly decimated by Rome. Nero, Caesar of Rome, sacrificed a swine on the temple altar of Jerusalem, the ultimate abomination. The temple was burned and torn down stone by stone. Jesus had said to the people that in their own lifetime, their enemies would come in and "not leave in you one stone upon another because you did not recognize the time of your visitation" (Luke 19:41-48). Thus came the end of the age, both of the Temple and of the kingdom of Israel. The internal kingdom of God, on the other hand, began to expand throughout the earth.

A new 'kingdom of priests' had been born. Individuals came to know and love the risen Christ and submit to His Lordship over their lives. This is the kingdom of God. Each individual has personal access to the king for forgiveness, direction, counsel, healing, comfort, provision and help. "The love of God was poured out in [their] hearts by the Holy Spirit" (Rom. 5:5). People who saw them could tell that "they had been with Jesus" (Acts 4:13). They became known as the ones "who have turned the world upside down" (Acts 17:6). Their love and care for each other regardless of class, gender or ethnicity was evident to those around them. The joy of the Lord was their strength.

As the new church grew, those Jews came to be called Christians by the general public and encountered severe and constant persecutions. Note the dramatic account of Stephen who was falsely accused of blasphemy before the Sanhedrin and who, after an eloquent oratorical defense, was stoned to death (Acts 6:8-7:60). Stephen, however, was distracted from his own execution by the grace of God in a revelation of the risen Jesus standing at the right hand of the Father to receive him into the heavenlies. One Saul of Tarsus, a devout leader of the Jews at the time, was in "hearty agreement" with this violence against Stephen. "And on that day a great persecution arose against the church in Jerusalem; and they all scattered throughout the regions of Judea and Samaria, except the apostles" (Acts 8:1).

This Saul, a highly educated man, was nonetheless provoked enough by the emergence of the new kingdom to be "breathing threats and murder against the disciples of the Lord" and the Christian believers evidently began to pray fervently to God concerning him. The resulting revelation of Jesus Christ that Saul received on the road to Damascus was unparalleled.

As Saul responded to Jesus that momentous day, the Lord changed his heart, and changed his name from Saul to Paul (Acts 9:1-25). He would never go back to being a leader of the Jewish religion again. He forsook all he had known and achieved to focus fully on what Jesus the Messiah was revealing to him. After an extended time of personal training in the Judean wilderness, Paul was sent by the Holy Spirit to preach also to the Gentiles, those who were not of Jewish origin (Gal. 2:1-10). Paul and his contingent began spreading the "good news" which they called the "Gospel" and starting church fellowships throughout the regions of Asia Minor and Macedonia.

As the Gospel was shared and preached in each of these places, those who believed gathered to learn about, worship, seek and serve the Lord Jesus together. As the love of God was manifested among them, they began to love and serve each other in unity and assist all those around them who were in need. The reality of a loving God was evident in their midst.

The remainder of Acts is the chronicle of this expansion. The Bible Epistles, Romans through Jude, are letters from Paul and the other Apostles to various churches and individuals. They include insight into and practical applications of the new-sprung kingdom of God addressing believers' motives, actions and attitudes, and teaching great wisdom to illuminate various areas of life. They contain instructions on how to live the Christian life in the face of the many persecutions and dilemmas the new believers faced. Their relevance to modern society is astonishing.

ULTIMATE VICTORY

The last book of the Bible is the end of the story. It is the Revelation of Jesus Christ to John the Apostle concerning who He is and what His plans are, and is a warning to God's people and to the world. In it is proclaimed the end of the cosmic story: "The kingdom of the world has become the kingdom of our Lord and of

His Christ; and He will reign forever and ever" (Rev. 11:15). The mustard seed kingdom has grown to engulf the whole garden; the leaven has leavened the whole lump of dough (Matt. 31:31-33). The conclusion of the work of God in human history is the triumph of Jesus and His kingdom in the affairs of men. This kingdom will have no end and those who have entered through repentance towards God and faith in the Lord Jesus Christ will be enjoying their King and each other forever. It will be heaven!

CHAPTER VII.

THE HAND OF GOD IN HISTORY IV

Pentecost to the Present

As we are able to trace the hand of God in His "inspired history" through the Bible, we can also trace the hand of God through the common facts and events of "recorded history." We will look at major individuals, events, institutions and documents that have driven the expansion of liberty through history to the present, as halting and bumpy as that expansion has been.

Studying what has happened historically shows what could happen in the future in any nation where Biblical principles are implemented as the moral and then structural basis of society. Every nation and people has a Christian history, the history of God's hand of grace fulfilling His historic purpose of liberty to the individual. This means that whoever we are, we must not be embittered and immobilized by the difficult past, but ask, "What has God been doing? Why am I here in this nation, in this culture, in this time? Why is the situation as it is? What should I do?"

We are not here by evolutionary accident. Life is too short to waste on bitterness over the past. The lesson of history is that God uses individuals to transform societies.

THE EARLY CHURCH

The church began at Pentecost as individuals came to know God personally through Jesus Christ by revelation of the Holy Spirit and gathered together to share their common experience with Him. They loved God and wanted to know Him. They loved each other and helped each other, meeting physical needs and providing spiritual and social support, reaching out to help those around them and sharing the Gospel with whomever they could.

As the new Christians drew near to God and gathered together with their friends for fellowship and encouragement, their natural abilities and the various gifts and callings of God channeled their activities in certain directions, some spiritual and some logistical (I Cor. 13). As certain individuals excelled in different areas of service toward one another, their functions were noticed and the local believers recognized them formally as leaders of those areas. Among these ministries, or areas of service, were apostles, prophets, pastors, teachers, evangelists, overseers, deacons and a host of other functions.

The apostles were the ones among the new church continually establishing new ministries, new ways to help the lost and bring them to Christ. The prophets were those who had the courage and boldness to confront the people about their sin. The pastors were the big-hearted members making sure everyone was included and felt at home. The teachers were trying to assist anyone they could to understand the faith properly. The evangelists were continually calling the people back to basic repentance and faith. The elders were working to organize things to be more effective. The deacons were taking care of the logistical details. In Christian terminology, this complex blend of relationships and service is metaphorically called "the Body of Christ."

Paul says, "There are no odd parts of the body" (I Cor. 12:18). I remember being in a meeting of campus ministry leaders at the University of Illinois. The question of the day was, "What things in your ministry cause you the most frustration?" I thought, "What I really want to do is study and teach, but I always have to do a lot of administration work that I can't stand." As the discussion got around to the person next to me, he said, "You know, I just like to make things run smoothly and get all the administrative details in order, but I always have to stop to teach!" At which I laughed and said, "I didn't know someone like you existed!" God has given gifts to the body as He has desired (I Cor. 12:11); we need each other, each fulfilling the roles and responsibilities He has given us and equipped us for.

SOMETHING NEW

As the early believers formally recognized these various avenues of service among them, the new, young gatherings became local self-governing fellowships, choosing their leaders on the basis of recognized servanthood and prayer. This was something new. Paul instructed Timothy in the epistles written to him concerning the basic requirements for overseers and deacons. There was no central human authority to which they looked for these decisions; they governed their own affairs, seeking God for direction and specifics.

Their structure once again looked like the structure in Fig. 5.2. Once again the individual is the servant of God, while the leaders serve the people and help them to know God, serve Him and govern themselves under Him. Authority flows from God to the individual and the people set up the structure by choosing representatives to lead them.

This is "bottom-up" government in that the power flow is from God to the individual at the "bottom" or base of the triangle, then "up" to the top or governmental structure through the choosing of representatives. In this model the people should have a mentality that asks "How would God want me to set up the structure to serve Him?" The leaders are those with recognized Christian character marked by humility and servanthood. By "set up the structure" we refer not only to the ordering of powers but also the question of what specific individuals should be placed into positions of authority.

The power flow in "top-down" government (Fig. 5.3) is from the ruling structure down to the individual to control and direct him, not leave him free and help him. In this model the mentality of both the individual and the leadership is that the individual is the servant of the structure, whether state or church.

The basis for liberty is Christian character. Liberty can come about, or work properly, only to the degree that the level of character in the people, society or institution is self-governing under God (doing right voluntarily) and takes on responsibility. This is why Paul did not write against slavery, but taught the principles of character that would eventually yield external liberty and abolish slavery on a global scale.

CONSTANTINE

In the first three hundred years of the church, the Gospel went throughout the Roman Empire. This was a time of extreme difficulty and hardship as the pride of the state came up against the conscience of the Christians. There were great persecutions as believers worked in obedience to Jesus' Great Commission to "Go into all the world and preach the Gospel to every creature" (Mark 16:15). To make matters worse there were heresies that were threatening the integrity of the faith. There was no printed Bible as such so the people needed their leaders for understanding when faced with these false new ideas.

Yet the church expanded over the years, each fellowship planting new fellowships, those fellowships going out to plant others and those youngest fellowships planting even more as illustrated in Fig. 7.1. Persecutions still increased over time, heresies still attacked the church, and as the geographical spread of the church increased, the churches slowly grew more and more dependent on their leaders, looking to them for wisdom and direction, and delegating to them increased powers. Fig. 7.1 is really a view of a developing top-down structure seen from above. This shift governmentally in mentality and structure from a network of self-governing fellowships to a centralized single, universal church was accompanied by a quality shift over the years from an internal personal religion to an external legal religion.

Roman emperor Constantine was converted in 312 AD and made Christianity not only legal but the favored religion of the Empire. Governmentally, he could look at the structure of the church, even tracing it back a century and see that it was basically a top-down configuration, the same as his empire. Reasoning that this must be God's way, he combined the state and the church, making this structure official. There were many good things that resulted, such as greatly diminished persecution, but one problem that developed was that the church began to "hire" its leaders based on qualifications other than spirituality. The church began to enforce its edicts with state power. This ultimately became a new church/state tyranny, as Israel had become in the days of the kings.

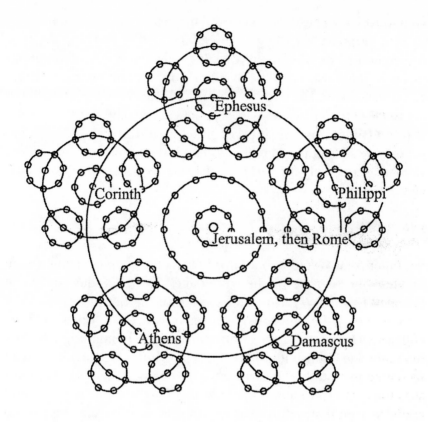

Fig. 7.1 The Church After Three Centuries

EUROPE

From Constantine's foundation, Christianity as a religion of Law spread through Europe and Scandinavia over the next 800 years. It came to be taught as a worldview throughout the region, though it was the remnant of new believers that came into a personal relationship with Jesus. If it were not for the Spirit of God bringing revival to His people through this time, as in every age, the church would certainly not have survived.

Through the centuries some important elements remained intact. The scriptures were copied in monasteries with absolute precision, preserving them for future generations. The Ten Commandments were taught as the basis for life. The understanding that Jesus was both true God and true man survived the years in the face of heresies to the contrary. The calling to spread the Gospel and help the poor surged and resurged. This is amazing considering that throughout this time there was no Bible available to the commoner. The Bible was accessible in Latin to the priests and leaders of the church, but not to the common person who was not educated in Latin. However, with no Bible, it is not surprising that distortions and abuses and oppression also cropped up in this church/state synthesis, even if one were to ascribe only the best of motives to God's people through the ages.

ENGLAND

Enter John Wycliffe, born in 1324. As the common people were "crying out because of their bondage" as in Exodus, the Lord revealed to John Wycliffe in his study of the Scriptures the very source of their liberty: self-governing character. Wycliffe and his colleagues began to translate the Bible into common English from the Latin and publish it (1382). They taught the people how to read so they could study the scriptures, and helped them reform their own lives. He carried out this task believing that one day it would result in a civil structure that would release liberty and a people who could maintain it.

Johannas Gutenberg was born in 1396 and began printing the Bible in 1455, accelerating the spread of the Bible to the masses. His movable-type printing press greatly expedited publishing while reducing the cost of printing Bibles. Martin Luther caught these ideas and asserted, "Each and all of us are priests." These were the most radical seven words uttered in centuries, proclaiming a new "kingdom of priests," the priesthood of all believers. Gutenberg's press multiplied these ideas. Luther referred to printing as "God's highest and extremest act of grace, whereby the business of the Gospel is driven forward." The ecclesiastical power structures, and the civil structures to which they were linked, shuddered at all this because it began to undermine their control.

By 1534, William Tyndale translated the Bible from the original Hebrew and Greek into English. Tyndale's translation was published under the name "Matthew Bible." His vision was simple. "If God preserves my life," he said, "I will cause a boy that driveth a plow to know more of the Scriptures than the Pope."[5] Tyndale came under intense persecution because King Henry VIII of England saw that if the people had Bibles, they would call his rule to account, weakening his power base. Finally, Tyndale was arrested and burned at the stake in a public square, 1535. He is said to have felt saddened at the thought of the king, who had already persecuted so many of God's servants and who remained obstinately rebellious against "that divine light which everywhere shone around him." His last words were, "Lord, open the King of England's eyes!" He was strangled and burned.[6]

Amazingly, within a year the King came to the conclusion that he could break England away from Rome if the people had access to the Bible! He wanted to break from Rome because the Pope would not grant him a divorce so that he could marry Anne Bolyn. He ran across a Matthew Bible. Tyndale's name was not in it, and the dedication to his Majesty was very well written. He came to a surprising decision: that a copy of this Bible should be placed in every church in England at the King's expense, and read daily to the people. It became known as the Great Bible (1539). Henry did it for his own personal ends, but God used him to get His word out. The people flocked to hear the word of God and began to look upwards to the Lord once again, individually coming into real relationship with God through Jesus Christ.[7]

In 1559, Biblical scholars who had been expelled from various parts of England and Europe for their reformation beliefs met in Geneva to translate yet another Bible. The "Geneva Bible" was divided into chapters and verses for the purpose of study. It was printed in Roman type to be more readable. It was affordable to a family. While previous Bibles had been folio size (approximately 18" by 24"), the Geneva Bible was quarto size (approximately 9" by 12") making it able to be carried. Revival began sweeping through Europe and personal reformation of character was following.

Then in 1611, still another version was published in England. It was a masterpiece of scholarship translated from the original languages into the common English of the day. It was sponsored and authorized by King James I and lacked any kind of notes, leaving interpretation completely free. This Bible became the standard and by 1901, the "King James Bible" had been translated into over 200 languages and dialects and 3 million copies per year were rolling off the English presses.

Meanwhile, internal government was being strengthened again, yielding a potential for external liberty and rocking the foundations of power.

A NEW ECCLESIASTICAL STRUCTURE

By the late 1570's in England, the common people had been exposed to the Bible for a couple of generations and many had come into a personal relationship with Jesus. As these lettered converts studied the Scriptures, they began to come under persecution from the state. They were doing things strictly forbidden — holding home Bible studies outside of the authority of the state church!

From the Scriptures, however, the believers could find nothing wrong with their activities. They were hungry to learn about the living God. Nonetheless, they were raided, imprisoned and relieved of their property by the authorities. The Christians saw this as unjust and began to clamor for the English church to be purified back to its original New Testament base. These Christians became known as Puritans. The battle was engaged as the power of the church/state combination came up against the conscience and courage of the Puritans.

In 1594, a group of Puritans in Scrooby, England came to the conclusion that the church/state looked more like the anti-Christ than an instrument of God. Finally, they reluctantly decided to break away from the Church of England altogether, forming their own self-governing church fellowship and beginning to reform their lives on their own. They studied the Scriptures to find out how to govern their own lives, their families, and their church. This was a radical move and they met with both persecution by the state and disapproval from their Puritan brethren. They were derisively called Separatists. But their conclusion was that the structure, civil or ecclesiastical, should exist to serve the individual, not rule the individual. So they set up a new structure in accordance with their belief that the individual is to govern himself in every area of life, including the ecclesiastical sphere. This decentralization was the result of an increase in self-governing character as they shouldered personal responsibility under God. This was the tiny, initial seed of local self-government.

ENGLISH SEPARATISTS IN HOLLAND

Under persecution, these separatists ultimately left England and went to Holland, where they spent ten years studying and working basically as slaves. It was very difficult because the separatists were farmers and the Dutch were sea traders and fishermen. The separatists had left virtually everything they owned behind when they left England, and were starting over. They hired themselves out as servants and soon gained a reputation for being hard workers, conscientious and honest, which put them in demand.

Beyond the physical difficulties was their grief over what had happened in England. They were God-fearing, honorable Englishmen yet had been hounded out of England by the church/state in authority there. Why, they wondered, would God allow this? What went wrong? During their ten years in Holland, they searched the Scriptures to find answers to these questions. They continued together as a local self-governing church, seeking God to learn how they should govern themselves ecclesiastically as well as personally.

Life was extremely difficult in Holland and ultimately they decided it would be better to go to the new world and take their chances there. Their leader, William Bradford, wrote of their reasons for this decision[8]:

1) Their situation entailed such difficult labor that few would join them in Holland and some could not stick it out.
2) They were beginning to age and needed to make a move before they were unable.
3) Their children's bodies were losing their vigor under the load, and though many had the best of dispositions, this grieved these Puritans.
4) Some of their children, as a result of the hardship and the "great licentiousness of the youth in that country" were

being drawn into Dutch sin and society, which grieved them even more.

5) They desired to "... advance the gospel of the kingdom of Christ in those remote parts of the world; yea though they should be but even as stepping stones unto others for the performing of so great a work."

Bradford wrote the history of the Scrooby congregation's wanderings in 1647, entitled "Of Plymouth Plantation." This is MUST reading for every American Christian. The vision, integrity, and fortitude of these people challenge us all and are a source of great encouragement and wisdom. Through their time of wandering they became known as Pilgrims.

In their Bible study during these years in Holland the Pilgrims came to seven great exchanges in philosophy of government:

1) From the idea of the infallibility of a church organization, to the idea of the infallibility of the Bible.

2) From the idea of political sovereignty belonging to King or Pope, to the idea of political sovereignty resting in the individual governed by God.

3) From the idea of sovereignty as being external, to the idea of sovereignty as being internal, God ruling in the heart of the individual.

4) From the idea of a class structure where the individual's value is based on external things (position, wealth, gender, race, age, ability), to the idea of equality for all where the individual's value is recognized as intrinsic, infinite and equal to every other person's value. Since all are treated by God as equal under His law, all must be treated by man as equal under civil law.

5) From the idea of limited freedoms of the individual as granted by the King, and therefore revocable by the King, to the idea of unalienable God-given rights of the individual to life, liberty and property.

6) From the idea of the flow of power in a nation being from the state to the people, thus making the individual the servant of the state, to the idea of the flow of power in a

nation being from the people to the state through the people choosing representatives, thus the state is the servant of the individual, the individual being the servant of God.

7) From the idea of compulsory uniformity in the externals in society to the idea of diversity with unity, recognizing the differences between people in gift, call and character, yet maintaining unity by virtue of equality of intrinsic value and our need for one another.

The Pilgrims set sail August 5, 1620 on two ships, the Mayflower and the Speedwell. The Pilgrims comprised half of the group on the Mayflower that left Europe for the New World. The rest were seafaring adventurers whom the Pilgrims called strangers. The voyage was long and bleak. They were 102 persons total, confined below for most of the voyage to an area the size of a volleyball court with a 5-foot ceiling. Severe storms blew them far off their intended course.

A NEW CIVIL STRUCTURE

Three attempts to sail to Jamestown, established nine years before by another group of Puritans in present day Virginia, were thwarted by weather. They finally put in at Plymouth on November 11 in present day Massachusetts, quite a distance removed from where they had expected to land. The place was cold and desolate, and very discouraging after their difficult voyage. The strangers recognized that they were not under any government here in the wilderness and threatened mutiny. Before going ashore, the Pilgrims drew up a government for the whole group known as the Mayflower Compact, given below from Bradford's history.[9]

The Mayflower Compact

"In ye name of God, Amen. We whose names are under-writen, loyall subjects of our dread soveraigne Lord, King James, by ye grace of God, of Great Britaine, Franc, & Ireland king, defender of ye faith &c., haveing under-taken, for ye glorie of God, and advancemente of ye Christian faith, and honour of our king & countrie, a voyage to plant ye first colonie in ye Northerne parts of Virginia, doe by these presents solomnly & mutualy in ye presence of God, and one of another, covenant & combine our selves togeather into a civill body politick, for our better ordering & preservation & furtherance of ye ends aforesaid: and by vertue hearof to enacte, constitute, and frame such just & equall lawes, ordinances, acts, constitutions, & offices, from time to time, as shall be thought most meete & convenient for ye generall good of ye Colonie, unto which we promise all due submission and obedience. In witnes wherof we have hereunder subscribed our names at Cap-Codd ye 11. of November, in ye year of ye raigne of our soveraigne lord, King James, of England, Franc, & Ireland ye eighteenth, and of Scotland ye fiftie fourth. Ano:Dom. 1620."

The purpose of this document was to define among them an authority by consent and to establish a promise to obey. It declares that as a civil body they will meet together to frame laws and ordinances needed for the good of the colony, and promise to obey them.

This one sentence marked the first time in history that men voluntarily established a civil form of self-government and agreed to it, both Pilgrims and strangers. It should be marveled that they knew just how to proceed. Actually they had been governing themselves as a church in this way for years, providing the model for the civil structure they now needed. Bradford said that they saw this act of theirs to be as secure as any patent granted by England, "and in some respects more sure."[10]

Some of the Biblical principles of government involved in the Mayflower Compact include these:

1) The individual has the responsibility to govern himself in every area of life and should be left free to do so.
2) The civil structure exists for protection, and the common good.
3) The civil structure exists to serve the individual, not vice versa.
4) Government must be by consent of the governed, not by decree from above.
5) All are equal under the law.

It should be noted that the Pilgrims approached their new relationship with the local residents, the Native American Indians, with these ideas in mind. They made a treaty with the Indians recognizing that the Indian was of equal value with the Englishmen and therefore was equal under the law, that there was no class difference between them, and that the purpose of the treaty was mutual protection, not control, to help the Indians not rule them. Both they and the Indians agreed to the treaty and lived in peace for more than fifty years.[11]

This was in contrast to the experience of the Puritans in Jamestown who had not yet arrived at the conceptual changes in their ideas of government. Though godly and sincere, the Virginia Puritans still possessed the traditional European ideas of government. They retained concepts of class structure, which viewed the value of the individual as defined by his station in life. They viewed the main purpose of civil government as control, rather than protection. Therefore they saw their duty as imposing government on the native peoples. The natives didn't appreciate this, and there was a good deal of trouble and bloodshed between them.

That first winter at Plymouth, meanwhile, found half of their number dead from hunger, disease and exposure. Yet when the Mayflower returned to England in the spring, none of the determined band of Pilgrims went back with it. They clung to the belief that God was doing something new. They believed that, in spite of the suffering they were enduring, they were in His will. This was truly a people of whom the world is not worthy.

A NEW ECONOMIC STRUCTURE

In the spring of 1621 the Pilgrims began to plant crops. God providentially placed a native Indian among them named Squanto who had traveled far afield to North Africa, lived in Spain with Christian monks, and learned to speak fluent English while visiting England. He was also familiar with the scriptures. Squanto taught them how to fish and plant corn, and was a liaison between them and the surrounding Indian tribes. Squanto had been prepared by God for fifteen years to help this band of Pilgrims get established in the new world.

As had been reluctantly agreed upon with the Merchant Venturers who financed their way, the Pilgrims' system of economics was to be "from each according to his ability, to each according to his need." This communal system, however, turned out to have crippling drawbacks. Those from the upper crust in England simply would not work the dirt. People would feign sickness. Attempting to force women and children to labor seemed tyranny to all. Some who worked felt it unfair. No one felt responsible for the fields to water, nurture and protect them from the wild animals through the summer. The result was that when harvest came, it was virtually non-existent. That fall and winter were very difficult. They spent their time foraging for sustenance, and some became servants to the Indians or sold them their blankets and goods, what little they had, for food.

In their distress again that winter they sought God for answers. They came to the conclusion that "*they should set corne every man for his owne perticuler*"[12], i.e. that each should govern his own life in the economic sphere as well.

When spring came, they did something new. They divided up the land and gave a piece of property to each family. They assigned single people to families, and gave each family a portion of the seed they had left. They basically said, "Here is your seed and there is your land. Do what you like with it."

Bradford says that since they were again facing starvation, everyone got right to work. The English upper classes, the women, the sick, the children, the pregnant were all out hard at work preparing the fields and planting seed. Each family nurtured its own piece of property through the summer. The result was that there was a plentiful harvest that second fall. Each family had enough to eat, store, replant and trade.

This was the seed of an individual enterprise system of economics, the application of Christian self-government in the economic sphere.

Bradford believed that the problem had been the system, not the people. He wrote,

> "The experience they had ... may well evince the
> vanity of that conceit of Plato and other ancients,
> applauded by some of later times; that the taking
> away of property, and bringing in community into a

common wealth, would make them happy and flourishing; as if they were wiser than God. For this
community (as far as it was) was found to breed
much confusion and discontent, and retard much
employment that would have been to their benefit
and comfort . . . And would have been worse if they
had been men of another condition. Let none object
this is men's corruption, and nothing to the course
itself. I answer, seeing all men have this corruption
in them, God in His wisdom saw another course
fitter for them."[13]

DEPENDENCE ON GOD

Bradford also notes, however, that lest they become dependent
on their new system, the Lord seemed to intervene against their
hopes of a crop,

"by a great drought which continued from the third
week in May, till about the middle of July, without
any rain, and with great heat (for the most part),
insomuch as the corn began to wither away ... part
wherof was never recovered. Upon which they set
apart a solemn day of humiliation, to seek the Lord
by humble and fervent prayer, in this great distress.
And He was pleased to give them a gracious and
speedy answer, both to their own and the Indian's
admiration, that lived among them. Though it was
hot through the morning and most of the day, toward
evening it began to grow overcast and then rain
gently in abundance without wind or thunder or
violence."[14]

It was an answer "as was wonderful to see, and made the
Indians astonished to behold."

Bradford says, "For which mercy (in time convenient) they also
set apart a day of thanksgiving."

Their first Thanksgiving Day was celebrated specifically for this answer to their prayer for rain as they humbled themselves before God. It was recognized as a feast of gratitude to God, who controls everything. Though they recognized that they had a system from God that could bring fourth abundance, it became evident to the Pilgrims that they still needed to recognize their daily personal dependence on God, just as the children of Israel had done in the wilderness they had faced, thousands of years before. We must acknowledge our dependence on God both for the system *and* for the working of the system.

THE PILGRIM'S CHARACTER

A couple of aspects of the Pilgrim's character should be mentioned since they are part of the spiritual heritage of America. In addition to the faith, steadfastness, self-governing, self-educating and entrepreneurial character already mentioned, there were clear expressions of faithfulness, charity and forgiveness to those who met and dealt with them.

There is no clearer example of these latter qualities than how the struggling colony at Plymouth dealt with those who had sponsored them in their quest to America. The English merchant venturers had financed the Pilgrim's voyage via the Mayflower at a usurious 40% interest. In return for this, the merchants had promised the Pilgrim settlers regular support shipments of food, tools, grain and other survival essentials. Instead, the unscrupulous merchants literally sent shiploads of freedom-seeking people, who were completely unprepared to deal with the harsh realities of life in the new world wilderness. As it turned out, the new arrivals were sent without personal provisions and the merchants neglected to include the support supplies they had promised the needy Pilgrims. Though betrayed by the English company several times, the Pilgrims arrived at the decision that they had contracted their voyage with the merchants in good faith and must keep their word and their end of the bargain. The Pilgrim settlement eventually paid off the entire sum with interest. This demonstration of the character of our forefathers is to us a precedent when tempted to default on financial agreements due to unjust, or even only irritating, treatment. The Bible instructed the early Americans to honor their word and contracts. The Pilgrims of the Plymouth colony saw this integrity as part of the spiritual roots of the new land.

The Pilgrims took in the new arrivals as their own and helped and taught them instead of turning them out to make their own way in the wilderness. This was at considerable strain to their own inadequate provisions and comfort. The Bible instructed them to love their neighbors as themselves, not mentioning circumstances. Jesus taught, "Whatever you wish others to do for you, do so for them." The context of this care was an attitude of forgiveness towards those in England who were using the new colony to line their own pockets.

God honored the Plymouth settlers. Over the years, the Pilgrims' ideas of character, civil government and economics became cornerstone foundations of the American political and economic systems. It took one hundred and fifty years of preparing the character of the colonists before God released them to break from England and become a nation. It also took the first Great Awakening to unite the colonists. The constitution of a land is first internal then external, first real individual character, and then the piece of paper.

The first Great Awakening in America took place in the period from approximately 1740 to 1780 when multitudes throughout the colonies came into a personal relationship with Jesus Christ in a true grass roots revival. It was a sovereign move of God, as He used the preaching of Wesley, Whitefield and Edwards. Along with an increase in personal righteousness came an understanding of God's ways in government by moral principle, and Biblical principles of civil government.

Rather than a general rebellion, the American Revolution was essentially a Biblical act of self-defense against increasingly unjust oppression by the mother country, as enumerated in the Declaration of Independence.[15] The Revolution had purpose and design, was carefully thought through, and was not simply anarchy against legitimate authority. In contrast, the French revolution's lack of this foundational base resulted in a reign of terror, anarchy and great arbitrary bloodshed.

A good exercise for every American Christian is to identify the Biblical principles in the Declaration of Independence and the Constitution of the United States. We must understand these ideas and be able apply them governmentally in order to survive as a free nation.

A BACKSLIDDEN NATION

As a nation, America has in our generation turned from God and we have ceased governing ourselves in various areas. We have been turning our freedom into license towards anarchy while at the same time becoming more dependent in character. The civil government has stepped in to take up the slack in education, welfare, health care, safety enforcement and other areas. This strengthens external government, eliminating freedoms and increasing the potential for corruption. We need revival in our land to turn this downward, tightening spiral around, strengthening internal government so that liberty can be restored and maintained.

CHAPTER VIII.

TWO VIEWS OF HISTORY

For the moment, let us go back in history to look at the growth of the church on a worldwide scale since its birth at Pentecost. This will show us the expansion of the internal component of liberty through the ages. External liberty is the *effect* of this internal liberty.

Dr. Ralph Winter, founder of the U.S. Center for World Missions in Pasadena, California, has been involved in compiling statistics about this growth. Truly, Jesus has been building His church and the gates of Hell have not prevailed against it (Matt. 16:18). The chart from USCWM in Fig. 8.1 is entitled <u>The Amazing Countdown Facts</u> and is a summary of those statistics. The graph in Fig. 8.2 gives an even clearer picture.

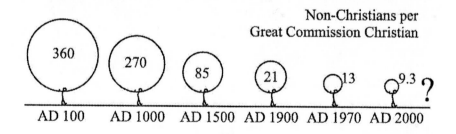

Just think! In AD 100 the number of people who did not claim to be Christians was 360 times the number of Great Commission Christians. That ratio has steadily dropped as the initiative of the Holy Spirit continues to outstrip our most optimistic plans!
USCWM

Fig. 8.1 The Amazing Countdown Facts

The church grew steadily as the Gospel went out from Jerusalem to fill the Roman Empire by 400 A.D., Europe by 800, and Scandinavia by 1200. As the Bible came into the hands of the "common" people, beginning in the 1400's with Gutenberg's printing press, missionary movements were spawned and we see a more rapid increase in the church. As maritime travel became more and more available, and then rail travel, the reach of the gospel increased worldwide. Finally, with air travel developing in the latter 1900's, we see an incredible exponential growth in the church. Dr. Winter states, "The initiative of the Holy Spirit continues to outstrip our most optimistic plans!" This is the world into which we were born.

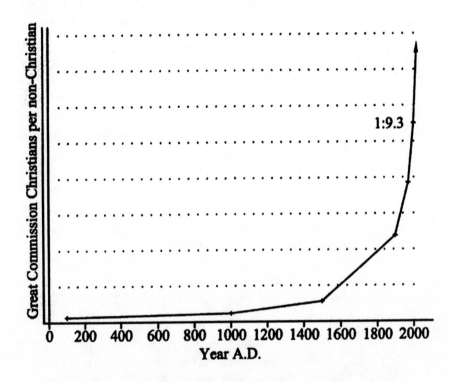

Fig. 8.2 Great Commission Christians Per Non-Christian

The graph in Fig.8.2 shows the ratio between Great Commission Christians and non-Christians since Pentecost. This is exciting because it takes into account population growth. The church is now growing three times faster than the population. Also, the term Great Commission Christian is a narrow category including primarily those Christians who take seriously the Great Commission. Thus, though 35% of the world's population call themselves Christians, only 15% would be categorized "Great Commission Christians."

Today, there are more than 400 mission agencies with plans to reach the whole world with the Gospel.

In 1983, Billy Graham gathered 6,000 itinerate evangelists in Amsterdam to train, encourage and send out afresh. In 1986, he gathered 10,000. These evangelists were from every nook and cranny on earth. In that context he made the statement that, "For the first time in history, accomplishing the Great Commission has become feasible in our generation." God is doing far more in the world that the devil is doing.

Since 1960, with air travel becoming easy and inexpensive, a whole new strategy of short-term outreach has begun. Virtually every mission agency today has programs to involve young people and average laymen in foreign missions outreach, distributing Scriptures, evangelizing, building, and encouraging local churches and missionaries worldwide.

All this is in combination with the working of God in response to today's vast international prayer movements.

The result of this increase in internal government is an increase in liberty. This takes time but is simply a consequence of an increase in character level.

At the same time, the devil is not taking this beating sitting down. He is using everything he can to kill, steal and destroy. He has particularly targeted the youth and the family since they are the most strategic areas. Now is no time for apathy, but time to use all our strength and resource to see the world evangelized and God's purpose in the world accomplished.

VIEW OF HISTORY

There are various worldviews concerning the direction and meaning of history. For instance, the Hindu view is that history is cyclical and will return to this point again in so many eons only to recycle again and again forever.

The Christian view of history is linear, stretching from eternity past to eternity future. God, Who always was, created the world at one point, is working out His purposes now, will conclude history on earth at some time in the future and then go on with His people forever. "But according to His promise we are looking for new heavens and a new earth, in which righteousness dwells" (II Pet. 3:13).

With this linear view of history in mind, there are two ways that Christians think about the direction of history. We will call them simply View A and View B, so that no denominations can be built on them. The first is shown in Fig. 8.3.

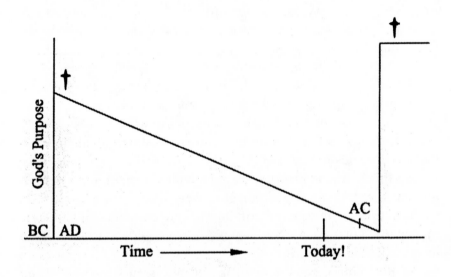

Fig. 8.3 Christians' View Of History A

The vertical scale on the left represents <u>God's purpose</u> and the horizontal scale below is <u>time</u>. View A sees things at their best at the time of Jesus and His resurrection and during the early church. The world has been going downhill since then and we are now at "Today!" The anti-Christ will arrive sometime soon. Then, just as things are approaching rock bottom, Jesus will return and carry on from there. At that time God's purpose on earth will be accomplished.

The other is shown in Fig. 8.4.

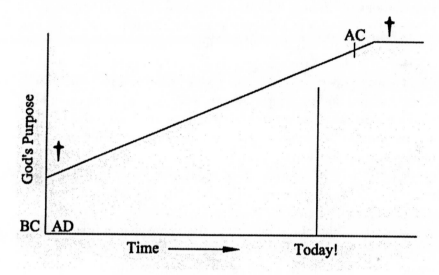

Fig. 8.4 Christians' View Of History B

View B is that God's purpose in history is liberty to the individual, first internal then external. God began His present age at the Incarnation, and internal liberty, God's kingdom reigning in individuals' hearts, has been increasing ever since. The consequence, external liberty, has also been increasing. We are now at "Today!" The anti-Christ will come at some point making a last-ditch attempt to salvage something, and Jesus will return and carry on from there.

These explanations are generalized, but many Christians in America hold to one or the other, many without having particularly thought about it. We want to look at the effect of each view on our mentality.

View B sees Jesus as Lord and His purpose being accomplished now over time. The prophesy concerning the Messiah in Isaiah 9:6 says, "...of the increase of His government and peace there will be no end." Jesus describes His kingdom as leaven that grows "until all is leavened." In Rev. 11:15 we see the angels rejoicing because "the kingdom of the world has become the kingdom of our Lord and of His Christ."

On the other hand, view A sees Satan's purposes being accomplished now, but Jesus will take care of him at some point in the future when He returns. This view sees us today in an unstoppable slide downward to destruction. As we read the morning paper and listen to the evening news, this view is reinforced daily. We know, however, that the Lord does not get much press.

Holding View A, our job as Christians is to get people saved — to get as many as possible off this sinking ship before it goes under. So evangelism and planting churches are what Christians should be doing, but working to reform the structures of society is not a valid occupation for Christians because reformation of society is seen to be impossible. It is futile; whatever is accomplished in this generation will only be overturned in the next. For many this has tended towards a short term, what's-the-use thinking when it comes to social concerns.

View B, on the other hand, says that there is real hope in Jesus Christ. The Christian's *first* job is to bring people to Christ, primarily because Jesus desires that restored relationship with them, but also because no real change can happen on earth unless the individual governs himself under God. Secondly, reformation of society is not only possible, but is *expected* as a result of people coming to Christ and growing in character; it is what God is doing. All true revivals change the structures of society. That reformation begins with the individual learning to apply the Bible in every area of his own life. Primary is Jesus' command to "Go into all the world and preach the gospel to every creature"(Mark 16:15). Following that is His command to "Occupy until I come"(Luke 19:13). This occupation is not merely to facilitate future evangelism, but also to change the structures of society to release liberty and peace and prosperity. God is grieved over the starving in India and the street orphans in Brazil, and wants the situation changed. We Christians have the answer. So in View B, evangelism is primary and work in society is valid for Christians.

Once I was giving a lecture on basic principles of government to a group of teachers at a Christian school. After a while, one of the teachers commented, "Bill, I know your life is committed to evangelism, but all this talk of working to change society is just not valid for Christians to be doing!" I was a bit surprised and asked her why she was teaching in a Christian school. She said thoughtfully,

"Well, I have to eat." Here was a wonderful Christian teacher who often went out on weekends to share the Gospel but didn't see her occupation, teaching children a Biblical education, as really valid. She saw her teaching as just a job, not a ministry or calling (vocation). This thinking tends to distract people away from occupations related to God's kingdom because there are a lot of jobs out there that bring in more money than teaching at a Christian school.

View B also tends towards a long-term mentality of building for your children's children's children, while view A tends towards a short-term mentality with respect to the future in things like savings, debt and long-range planning. It also colors questions like "Should I spend four years in college?" This decline becomes self-perpetuating as we reach the future unprepared.

Young Christians ask, "Is it valid to spend all this time in college while so many are still lost and there is no time left?" View B would indicate that there *is* time left and that college is a valid pursuit if God directs. The field of evangelism would be the college campus for now and then the rest of the world later, as He leads.

Another result of view A is a question that I have heard and even asked personally myself, "Is it morally right to marry and bring children into this terrible world?" The answer in our heart is "Of course!" but in our minds, we struggle. The answer according to view B is, "Yes! Yes! Yes!" God is into life. We haven't filled the earth yet. God has a plan and is accomplishing it. There has never been a better time to marry and have children, especially in the Western World. Not only is there hope in Jesus, but there is more hope now for the world then ever before.

Actually, instead of looking like the straight line shown in Fig. 8.4, view B looks like the exponential curve in Fig. 8.2. The fulfillment of God's purpose is increasing exponentially at this point in history, not just linearly. Worldwide, the church is growing faster today than ever before. This is the advance of internal liberty.

The advance of external liberty follows. There's a big job for us to do. God has a destiny for this generation. All we must do is walk in it. Each of us has an absolutely significant part.

View B was the view the Pilgrims had when they sailed to the New World. They knew that God was building something for the future and that they had a significant role to play in it, even though they would not experience it themselves. They were building even though someone else would reap the blessing. Though half of them died the first winter, none of them returned to England in the spring. I marvel at these people. I think that if half of my team died the first year, I'd probably conclude that I was out of the will of God.

BOTH EVANGELISM AND REFORM

View B, which recognizes both evangelism and reform, was the predominant view in America until the mid-19th century. Charles Finney's ministry, 1825-1875, is a good example of this combination of responsibilities. While he preached powerful revival, bringing thousands back to their first love for Jesus, he also preached against the evils of slavery, helping fuel the drive for its abolition. He preached against discrimination from the Biblical moral basis of equality of intrinsic value. Discrimination on the basis of race is wrong. So is discrimination on the basis of gender. Finney founded Oberlin College, the first to admit African Americans and women. The Bible is the place where a solid philosophical basis for equality and justice can be found.

William Booth is another example. His Salvation Army, which spanned the globe, saw helping the poor as the back of the coin of preaching the Gospel.

In the mid-19th century, however, there came a shift in perspective as the advent of Higher Criticism in Germany claimed to debunk the supernatural in the Bible, and the publishing of Darwin's Origin of Species called into question the creation story and introduced evolution into mainstream thought. The church didn't know how to respond to this onslaught. The Civil War's cruelty was also a disillusioning factor at this time. Part of the church accepted these ideas and began to shift to a naturalist position, deciding that the world is falling apart and the Christian's task is to improve society and help man evolve. In response to this "social" gospel, the evangelical church said, "No, since the world is falling apart the Christian's task is to save people out of the world instead of improving it," and began to lose its vision for reform. A set of papers was published in the early 20th century called The Fundamentals which did a good job of defending the fundamentals of the faith — the authority of Scripture, the creation story, the virgin birth, the divinity of Christ, the resurrection of Jesus, the necessity of personal salvation, etc. These "fundamentalists" focused on evangelism as the Christian's task, but came to see social reform as diversion.

Since the 1950's there have been revival movements in liberal churches that are restoring the emphasis on personal relationship with God through Jesus Christ and the authority of Scripture, as well as evangelism. There has also been recognition in the evangelical churches of our need to love our neighbor as well as love God, restoring the emphasis on reform and meeting people's temporal needs along with spiritual needs.

Social change to liberty instead of anarchy cannot happen without a foundation of evangelism and self-governing character. The result of these theological shifts was a social gospel that eventually left out evangelism altogether seeing it as unnecessary, and the reaction was an evangelical gospel that virtually left out social reform altogether, seeing it as invalid for the church and a basic waste of time and resources. The Gospel of Jesus Christ is a two-handed Gospel, however, evangelism then social change, loving God and loving our neighbor as ourselves. Having a family, reforming the structures of society, getting a college education are all valid for Christians as God directs, alongside world evangelism.

I have a friend who led an evangelism team in Belo Horizonte, Brazil. As his team went out into the jungle to share the Gospel, they kept finding abandoned children. The team took them in and soon had an orphanage as part of their ministry. He began to see, however, that orphanages were not the long-range solution to the problem of the millions of street orphans in Brazil. Besides the enormity of the numbers, even though the orphans' physical and emotional needs may be somewhat met in the orphanage, they will still have a difficult time eventually raising their own children, not having any model. The long-range solution was first a widespread, prevalent moral change within the family toward God and love and faithfulness and courage, and then a political/economic change that would provide opportunity for the family's economic advance. He went back to university to begin pursuing this long-range solution in addition to the immediate need of providing orphanages. This was added to the primary task of evangelism.

In all of this our need is to get back to the Bible as the basis of all of life.

THE RETURN OF CHRIST

Though there are various theories about when He will return, Jesus Himself told us, "It is not for you to know times or epochs which the Father has fixed by His own authority; but you shall receive power..." (Acts 1:8). He did not come in 1948, or 1988.

It is not for us to know.

One thing we do know: Jesus told us "Yes, I am coming quickly" (Rev. 22:20).

He also told us "But of that day no one knows, not even the angels of heaven nor the Son, but the Father alone" (Matt. 24:36).

This is because of the great mercy of God: "But do not let this one fact escape your notice, beloved, that with the Lord one day is as a thousand years, and a thousand years as one day. The Lord is not slow about His promise [of judgment], as some count slowness, but is patient toward you, not wishing for any to perish, but for all to come to repentance. But the day of the Lord will come..." (II Pet. 3:8-10).

Since He may return tomorrow, we must always be ready in character to meet Him. "And while [the foolish virgins] were going away to make the purchase, the bridegroom came, and those who were ready went in with him to the wedding feast; and the door was shut" (Matt. 25:1-13). This is not a problem when borne out of a love relationship with God.

On the other hand, since it may be another thousand years until He returns, we must also be ready in our building and planning for that possibility, and faithfully occupy until He comes.

CHAPTER IX.

CHRISTIAN VS. PAGAN VIEWS OF MAN AND THE STATE

Who is the servant of whom?

Government is defined as "that flow of power which controls the actions of the individual." While God is sovereign and the ultimate source of authority, men choose who will rule their lives. We make this choice by submitting ourselves in trust and obedience.

The media has such power and authority because people submit to it in trust. Many feel that anything we see on TV in living color on the news is true. Anything printed in the newspaper is true. This is not necessarily the case. The people who write or shoot the news stories have limited ability, have a limited understanding of what is going on and have presuppositions that define their interpretation of the facts. Some may even have an agenda they are accommodating.

PRINCIPLE: People choose who or what will rule their lives.

THE PAGAN VIEW OF MAN AND THE STATE

The pagan view of man and the state is that the individual is the servant of the state, as shown in Fig. 9.1. God has overall sovereignty, but since the individual does not submit himself to God, he is dependent on man, and finally the state.

The governing flow of power is from the state to the individual. This is external government. In the extreme case, the state educates the individual, provides for him, decides what the church may teach and do, decides what vocation the individual will have and controls the media, the arts and the news. It even decides how many children a family will have, where the family will live, where they may travel and even what they may wear. The state totally controls the life of the individual. The purpose of the individual is to serve and support the state. The state uses any and every means to increase its power and effectiveness, "for the good of the people" of course.

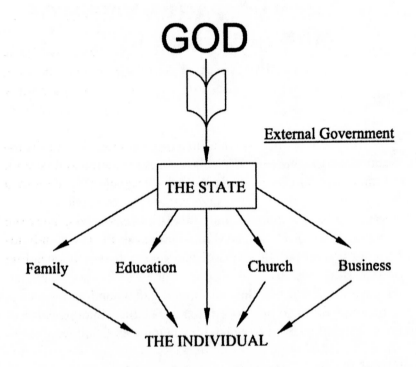

Fig. 9.1 The Pagan View Of Man And The State

This is the case in many nations today: Communist countries, right-wing dictatorships and Islamic dictatorships most notably. This was the case in Egypt under Pharaoh in Exodus. The character of the people is one of dependence. In America, our freedoms are eroding as character declines and the people demand a "king."

This can begin to change as people look to God, repent of their sins, place their trust in Jesus and submit themselves to Him and His word, the Bible.

As people come to Christ and are saved, changes begin to

happen. First, they start reforming their own lives according to God's word. They stop murdering, stealing, committing adultery, rebelling against parents, defaulting on contracts and coveting what belongs to others. The love of God is placed in their hearts (Rom. 5:5) and their lives begin to exhibit the fruit of the Spirit: love, joy, peace, patience, kindness, goodness, gentleness, meekness and self-control (Gal. 5:22). Against such things there is no law. They cease to be on the wrong side of God's law. They begin to govern their own lives under God.

Then they notice that there are others around who love Jesus and are in the same situation, needing encouragement and nurture. So they gather together as a group to help each other. As they study the Bible they learn how to govern themselves in their fellowship together.

Next they notice that the Bible has things to say about governing their family relationships: husband to wife, wife to husband, parents to children, children to parents. They begin to see how a family was meant to be.

They are involved in businesses and financial matters. They see that God's word has standards and wisdom in this area. The individual is to govern himself in the economic sphere also, not depending on the state, but on God.

Next, the individual's children must be educated. He does not want his children to grow up not knowing God and dependent or rebellious in character as he did, so he searches the Scriptures with respect to his kids' education. Here he finds out that education is the responsibility of the family, not the state. What to do — public school, Christian school, home school? He must govern himself in this area, too.

The media is affecting him and his family. How does he govern their influences? The most effective way to govern the influence of the television is perhaps to drop it over a cliff, admittedly external.

There are poor people around him. The Bible says that helping them is the responsibility of the church, not the state.

There are many other areas about which he must also ask God concerning vocation, direction in life, service to others, etc.

Finally, the Bible says that civil government has proper tasks and boundaries and is to be structured to remain confined to these boundaries. The people must govern themselves in this area, too, deciding what kind of civil structure will best accomplish these functions and then choosing/hiring people to do this work for them, limiting their power to just what is authorized by Scripture.

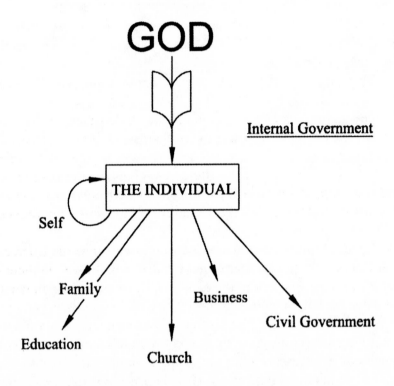

Fig. 9.2 The Christian View Of Man And The State.

So over time, we see the Christian view of man and the state emerge in Fig. 9.2. The state is the servant of the individual and has specific limited functions. The individual is the servant of God and is to govern himself according to God's law and word and ways in every area of life.

He is free!

We can construct a relative scale between the pagan view of man and the state and tyranny, and the Christian view of man and the state and liberty, illustrated in Fig. 9.3.

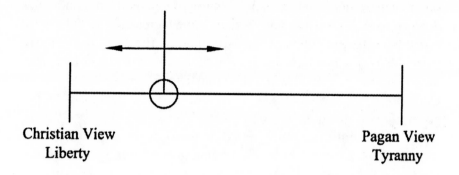

Christian View
Liberty

Pagan View
Tyranny

Fig. 9.3 Freedom/Slavery Scale

Every nation and society would be located at some point on that scale. That point is defined by the character of the people. That nation or society is also moving on that scale towards liberty or tyranny depending on whether Godliness and self-governing character are increasing or decreasing.

It seems that America is positioned more towards liberty but moving towards tyranny as character declines. In Russia there has been an external advance in freedom. It remains to be seen whether the character of the people there will result in a long-term increase in liberty or a lapse back into tyranny. A dependent people with the vote will elect stronger rulers into office; a Godly people will elect restrained leaders into office.

Starting with a situation of much liberty in Fig. 9.2, what happens if the people fall away from God, if God begins to fade in their hearts over the years? As dependence on God decreases, dependence on the state increases and the power flow begins to invert.

First, personal righteousness begins to seem not so important; apathy is an effect of liberty and ease. Then money becomes the bottom line, the husband sacrificing wife and kids on the altar of "Things." The next generation sacrifices the kids on twin altars of "his Things" and "her personal Rights." The integrity of the family becomes secondary. The embittered kids grow up increasingly ungoverned and anarchistic as the state is given full reign to educate them. God's people, the church, cease taking care of the poor, shifting that authority upwards to the state. Church becomes another social club, religious but with no mention of the Ten Commandments or a personal relationship with Jesus. Crime increases. Candidates for office become judged by "who will give me the most if I vote for them," disregarding character altogether. As those in power lavish tax money on the people to win votes, they can do anything they want. Corruption increases. Taxes increase. Liberty decreases. Civil government is given increasing power.

At this point this society *must* come to its senses. The people must turn back to God individually and govern themselves according to the Bible in every area, taking on corresponding responsibility. Otherwise, loss of freedom will ensue and tyranny will arise, perhaps for generations.

CHAPTER X.

PRACTICAL APPLICATION

The Spheres of Christian Self-Government

Where do we begin in our learning to think governmentally and apply practically the ideas and principles of Christian self-government? Let's look at some of the various issues, relationships, spheres of government and courses of action we are involved with on a day-to-day basis. There are Christians working at reform in each of these areas and many more, compiling vast resource materials and creating opportunities for involvement. While we each have responsibilities in all these areas, God may be calling us to emphasize one particular area in our own life and ministry.

SPHERE I. SELF

The first sphere of government for which we are responsible is the personal sphere. Not someone else's person, but my own. It's easy to say, "Yes, that person needs to get with it," or "Yes, they need to hear this." Rather, we must say, "I must change. Lord, have mercy on *me*. Lord, help me reform my life." It begins in our own individual hearts. And by the grace of God, we can be changed.

The first area is personal righteousness, keeping away from sin. This beginning step is foundational to all else. Its basis is the moral law found in the Ten Commandments in letter, and the Sermon on the Mount in spirit. It is summed up in one word: love (Matt. 22:34-40, I Cor. 13, I Tim. 1:5). This love is not a feeling or emotion, but seeking the highest good instead of personal gratification and advancement. This love is our chosen motive in life rather than self-centeredness. It is the love of God.

God's purpose in the individual's life is that he becomes "conformed to the image of Christ" (Rom. 8:28). God loves us and will spare nothing to accomplish that purpose. He says, "Oh, that they had such a heart in them, that they would fear Me and keep My commandments always, that it may be well with them and with their sons forever" (Deut. 5:28-29) and "Oh, that My people would listen to Me, that Israel would walk in My ways! I would quickly subdue their enemies, and turn My hand against their adversaries ... And with honey from the rock I would satisfy you" (Ps. 81:13). These words show the great heart of God towards us. Listening to God, fearing God and obeying God lays a foundation for strength of character.

Solomon admonishes to "Remember also your creator in the days of your youth..." (Eccles. 12:1). We should start now and not wait.

Then, too, there are various areas of discipline in which we need to learn to govern ourselves; some are spiritual and some temporal. These areas include:

Knowing God — This is the foundation of all of life. The purpose of life is to know God. This is what we were created for. Spend time with Him daily. Knowing God is the source of strength and wisdom and courage.

Studying God's word, the Bible — The Bible is the revelation to man of God and His ways. It contains the answers to all facets of life. Read through the Bible each year. Research the areas and topics that fascinate you. Apply what you learn personally and in your sphere of influence.

Prayer — This is a part of knowing God. Learn all aspects of prayer: "seeking prayer" to know Him not just "asking prayer" to receive from Him; intercessory prayer which is prayer for others; seeking God for direction and wisdom; building and using a daily prayer list.

Personal grooming and health — Keep up personal grooming and hygiene. This is necessary personal maintenance and mercy on those around us. You are the temple of God.

Family — It is the ministry of every child to bring joy to the hearts of his parents. Children can bring blessing, help and joy to the family, learning to take initiative and doing chores without being asked. This is practice in self-government. Parents give time, nurture and support. Each family cares for its own aged. This is the first sphere of government.

Personal evangelism — Schedule a time often for personal witnessing, sharing the Gospel with someone who doesn't know Jesus. This is expanding God's internal kingdom and is prerequisite to any other solid social change.

Job/ministry/school — "And whatever you do in word or deed, do all in the name of Lord Jesus, giving thanks through Him to God the Father" (Col. 3:17). Whether you are a student, minister, laborer or "whatever you do," do it for Jesus. Diligence, integrity and thankfulness are key. Serve and do your best even though no one but Jesus may see.

Finances — Keep up tithing, stay out of debt, get organized and be generous. This is practice in faithfulness. As we are faithful in the small things, God will release greater things.

Missions — Help bring the Gospel to the world through prayer, supporting missions activities financially and being personally involved in the Great Commission. Go on a regular basis on some of the many short-term outreach programs available. World evangelism *now* is essential.

Maintenance — Keep property and vehicles maintained. This is a string of chores but they must be done in order not to be wasteful of God's resources. Maintenance is just a part of owning property.

All this requires faithfulness.

Then there are areas of study, ministry and meeting needs in which we may be gifted and/or called by the Lord, full-time or part-time:

Family Ministry
Evangelism/Missions
Education, Christian or Public
Business
Mercy ministry/Refugee ministry
Media
The arts and entertainment
Civil government
The poor

There are also problem areas in society that need reform: pornography, abortion (legal, education, and alternative aspects) and prisons for example.

God's first commandment is that we love Him with all our heart, soul, mind and strength. As Christians, we need spiritual development (heart), character development (soul) and intellectual development (mind). One can develop self-educating character by cultivating the habit of reading books regularly, perhaps one per month. At that rate, in ten years he will have read 120 books about his favorite area of interest, along beside his Bible study. He will be an expert in that area. There are vast, excellent resources available in any field of study.

All of this builds a foundation and context for vocational development (strength). This is a life of service to God and others in whatever vocation God chooses. The word 'vocation' means 'calling,' and God has a calling or vocation for each individual for which He trains, tests, develops and releases him. Our work has actual value because it is our own expression of God's creativity and reflects His handiwork. This vocational development includes improving the quality, effectiveness, efficiency, beauty and service of our work. This applies to the eloquence of a teacher or preacher, the craftsmanship of a factory worker or carpenter or the courage of an entrepreneur or missionary. We are "...rendering service, as unto the Lord, and not to men," (Eph. 6:5-8).

As we put what we learn into practice in service, we will grow in our understanding and authority and can be a great influence for righteousness. We must seek the Lord for His direction since He is sovereign and has the plan. We can begin afresh now.

SPHERE II. FAMILY

The second sphere of government is the family. If God is sovereign in the individual's life, then the first external arena that He has delegated to the individual to govern under Him is his/her marriage and family.

We must be careful to keep our own marriage and family intact. This is first internal, then external. First is our commitment and affection towards our spouse. Marriage is more than living together externally while living apart internally. It is a love relationship, each living for the other instead of for self. It is not a 50/50 arrangement but a 100/100 partnership. For a marriage to produce the blessing God intended, a couple must be bound together in Jesus, not in things, children, security, sex or status. The pressure is always to substitute the superficial (career, fulfillment or things) for the valuable (relationship and faithfulness). Resisting this pressure builds character. Giving up is apathy.

If we presuppose there is no God and that man evolved by chance, then the term "family" is defined by men. If that is the case, we look around and see what people think about the family, look into history to get a larger perspective and vote on what the definition for family will be. Typically, those who have the loudest, most forceful voices win the vote. In our day, those who control the media tend to win the vote. We also can vote again in the next generation if we want to redefine it.

If, however, God exists and is sovereign and created the family, then He is the one who has given the family its definition, purpose and function. The Bible presents a simple definition of the family: a man, his wife and their children. So family is an absolute term, not a relative term that changes from age to age and society to society. As we stray away from God, our human definitions add more and more confusion to the subject.

The family is where parents learn to govern and children learn to be governed. The purpose of marriage is relationship, not personal security or getting selfish needs fulfilled. The purpose of the family is to train the next generation in Godly, self-governing, non-dependent character.

The husband is the head of the house and of his wife (Eph. 5: 23). What does that mean? Biblically, God is sovereign in the wife's life as well as the husband's. The wife and the husband are of equal intrinsic value and are to live that way. Jesus told us that the greatest authority will be the greatest servant. The job of the husband, then, is not to rule his wife, but to serve her with protection and to release her into all God has for her. The wife is to serve him, helping him perform this function and releasing him into all God has for him. They are to move forward together. In Eph. 5:23-33, the model of the husband's relationship to his wife is that of Christ to the church.

The relationship of the wife to her husband is that of the church to Christ. This is a two-way, non-selfish, active love relationship.

Looking at the sovereignty grid, if we presuppose that God does not exist then our view on the left is that both husband and wife are autonomous and equally sovereign. This does not make for relationship, since harmony in this case exists only to the extent that they stay out of each other's lives. Our view on the right is that the structure is sovereign and is to exercise its power to gain obedience externally, which is harshness. As men have opted for the first, they have abdicated their responsibility, leaving their wives to fend for themselves. As they have opted for the second and become tyrants in the home, they have driven their wives away.

Our culture is full of embittered wives who have not been protected on the one hand, or have not been released but held down on the other. Both problems have spawned rebellion and driven the family apart.

SOVEREIGNTY GRID - MARRIAGE RELATIONSHIP

left extreme Presupposition: God does not exist.	Biblical Presupposition: God exists.	right extreme Presupposition: God does not exist.
Individual is sovereign.	God is sovereign.	Structure is sovereign.
Husband and wife equally sovereign but autonomous.	Husband & wife equal value, husband authority through servanthood.	Husband is sovereign; wife is slave.
Anarchy: each has own direction.	Servanthood: working together.	Tyranny: husband is absolute authority.
Center is *me*: "You must change."	Center is *God* and *you*: "I must change."	Center is *husband*: "You obey me."
No relationship: freedom but empty.	Love relationship: working together.	Obedience relationshp order but sterile.

Jesus said that servanthood is the key to true authority. Servanthood is self-sacrifice, actively helping each other to reach a common goal, in this case a love relationship. Servanthood is not being a doormat. As both husband and wife strive to be the greatest servant, they increase their authority in their spouse's life.

Problems come when one spouse turns to self-centeredness, not servanthood, and his or her authority diminishes in their spouse's life. This rejection can open the door to a third party intrusion, whether a person, a job, a hobby, ministry, the kids or even food.

In times of conflict both spouses on the left see the other person as the problem and think that it is the other person who needs to change. There is no solution to this until someone yields, a difficult prospect. On the right, the problem is obedience according to the husband and bossiness according to the wife. It is felt the only solution is for the wife to obey, but she feels compromised.

The Biblical solution to conflict is for both husband and wife to recognize what a love relationship is and that the center of the world is not himself or herself but the other. Each must recognize that he or she is not in this relationship for his or her own fulfillment, but to fulfill the other. Each must recognize the need for his own personal change, not think it is the other who needs to change. Each should pray, "God change me," instead of "God change him" or "God change her." This gives a basis for building a loving relationship. Each of us is only actually in charge of our own life.

If one is not born again, however, he cannot see the kingdom of God and this doesn't make sense.

THE CHILDREN

Let us add children to this marriage. Our view of sovereignty will influence our purpose in having children and our methods in raising them. Since the family is where the individual learns to govern himself, it is of utmost importance. That which works against the family (remember family is an absolute term) undermines society and moves it towards tyranny. The government inside the home will produce a character and mentality in the next generation that will be either capable of sustaining liberty or dependent on external control.

SOVEREIGNTY GRID - THE FAMILY

left extreme	Biblical	right extreme
Presupposition: God does not exist.	Presupposition: God exists.	Presupposition: God does not exist.
Individual is sovereign.	God is sovereign.	Structure is sovereign.
Anarchy. no gov't.	Liberty with law. internal gov't.	Tyranny. external gov't.
Parental libertinism, no authority. No law, only affection. Absolute freedom.	Godly authority, servanthood. Love ruling by law. Maximum freedom.	Parental despotism, absolute authority. Absolute law, no love. Minimum/no freedom.
Parents do not provide law or guidance: permissive home. No character developed; obedience non-existent.	Parents develop God's law for the home: training -- love with law. Self-governing character; obedience internal.	Parents have power over life of child: despotic home. No character developed; obedience external.
Child ignorant of law, sees obedience as needless.	Child values law, sees obedience as good.	Child hates law, sees obedience as compromise.
Child develops disrespectful familiarity by parent doing nothing.	Child develops proper fear with love by parent training and leading.	Child develops slavish fear by parent forcing obedience without love.
Produces no penitence due to ignorance. Produces hatred of self.	Produces penitence: reform of heart & conduct. Produces hatred of offence.	Produces no penitence due to slavish obedience. Produces hatred of authority and law.
Prepares for anarchy -- no law or reasoning. Child can be manipulated by peers. Leads to hedonism, secularism.	Prepares for Christian self-government -- Law with reasoning. Child cannot be manipulated. Leads to freedom and safety.	Prepares for tyranny -- law, no reasoning. Child can be manipulated by authorities. Leads to cults, media and other elite control.

If we view the individual as sovereign, then the child is also sovereign in and of himself, as are his parents. Here, in the extreme, parents do not provide law or guidance but let the child do what he feels like doing. Forcing law on a child is seen as cruel. Family government becomes parental libertinism: no authority or law, only affection. In this permissive home, the child does not learn to submit to authority or others and becomes incapable of governing himself. There is no character development; obedience is non-existent. The bond in this family is feelings.

On the other hand, if we view the structure as sovereign, we have parental despotism, many times as a reaction to permissiveness. Here parents have absolute authority, exercising absolute law without love. Not exercising total control over the child is seen as detrimental. So the child obeys, but as a slave obeys in a mechanical dependence on external control. There is no character development here either; obedience is only external compliance. The bond in this family is fear.

The Biblical alternative is to exercise God's authority through servanthood. This will include sanctions for behavior along with training and love. A child must grow up knowing at the deepest level that there are consequences to actions. The goal is to help the child to know God and to govern himself under God. Here we have love with law, a love that is more than affection. It is a love that teaches the child God's law (not just arbitrary rules) and trains him to obey it out of conviction, seeing obedience to God as intelligent. Here, the child learns to submit voluntarily to Godly home government and is therefore free. He develops Godly self-governing character; obedience is internal. The bond in this family is love.

While in the permissive home the child is ignorant of the law and regards obedience as needless, and in the despotic home the child comes to hate the law and regards obedience as a compromise of true liberty, in the Godly home the child comes to love the law and regards obedience as the highest good.

While the permissive home develops a disrespectful familiarity with authority by the parents not providing direction, and the despotic home develops mechanical servitude by forcing compliance, the Godly home must produce a *proper* sense of fear and respect for authority by training and leading.

While the permissive home produces no penitence due to ignorance, and the despotic home produces no penitence due to a developed hatred of authority, the Godly home must strive to produce penitence and reformation of both heart and conduct, and a hatred of the offense as the child learns the stupidity of sin.

With respect to religion, in the permissive home the child is left free to choose his religion, or no religion at all. Assuming here that God does not exist, it really doesn't matter. In the despotic home, the child is told what to think. This is regarded by the child as a compromise of his liberty and ultimately produces rebellion.

The Godly home focuses on nurture, admonition, prayer and reasoning. Heart response and internal character are the goals. The parents set the example with love and righteousness.

Finally, the permissive home prepares the individual for blind anarchy. He does not learn law or reasoning. The despotic home prepares the individual for blind dictatorship. He learns compliance to law, but not reasoning. The Godly home prepares the individual for Christian self-government. He learns law with reasoning, obeying law because it is the highest good, yet not blindly.

The result of the permissive home is rebellion and hedonism, and a person who can be manipulated by his peers and colleagues. The result of a despotic home is a person who can be manipulated by authorities. He is dependent and senses a need for someone to tell him what to do. This opens him up to cults and other controlling authorities.

The goal of Christian parenting is to raise children in such a way that the shift is complete from total dependence, ignorance and self-centeredness at birth to independence, intelligence and righteousness when the child leaves the nest. The child must be able to stand on his own and must be immune to manipulation from either his peers around him or the many authorities screaming at him. He must know what he believes and why he believes it, be able to figure out what is right and be able and motivated to do it. A Godly self-governing people will be free.

This character is not an accident, but the result of training. Children do not inevitably have to rebel. This is good news.

SPHERE III. THE CHURCH

The next sphere of government is the ecclesiastical sphere - the church. We can look at two aspects, attitude and structure. Attitude is the mentality and character of the people and the leadership. Structure is the mechanics and specific organization of the church body.

In attitude, the church leadership and structure exist to serve the individual, not the individual to serve the local church. The purpose of the church leadership is to provide spiritual protection, and to train Godly conscience in the people so they can follow God and govern themselves under Him.

The church is after all, just people assembling together to love Jesus, who then select/elect/appoint/hire individuals to perform particular functions among them: pastor, board member, Bible study leader, elders, deacons, etc.

The challenge is for everyone to look to the Lord and grow in relationship with Him and in character, decreasing in dependence on man. The challenge for the individual is to take initiative in his spiritual walk. The challenge for the leaders is to assist the individual to fulfill God's plans in his life. The temptation is to attempt to force this process, but any coercive attitude builds character that is dependent on the church rather than dependent on God.

Like raising a child, developing a new Christian involves a painstaking process of shifting him, or her, from spiritual helplessness to spiritual maturity. He or she must move from habits of selfishness to habits of holiness, from dependence and ignorance to non-dependence and wisdom. There are stages in this growth:

> infant - bonding stage - needs love
> toddler - concrete stage - needs law
> youth - training stage - needs discipline
> adolescent - self-government stage - needs reason & freedom
> adult - liberty stage - needs freedom with counsel

When a person first comes to Christ, he needs simply to know that God loves him. Like an infant child needs to be cuddled, the baby Christian needs to be encouraged and reassured. As he grows older, in the toddler stage he needs concrete rules from the discipler. "Yes, do this. No, don't do that." As he grows into the youth stage, he begins to learn how to serve the Lord and especially why, digesting everything his leaders teach him. Coached through adolescence, he learns to stand on his own in the freedom of the Lord and make right choices when faced with temptations. By maturity, the initiative for discipleship has shifted from the discipler to the disciple. The disciple is fully able to seek God himself, obey Him and lead others. The speed at which an individual grows in the Lord depends on his willingness to yield to God's will all along the process.

Problems occur if the latter stages of this process are truncated and at the youth stage the disciple remains dependent on his elders instead of learning to take the initiative to govern himself under God. This occurs when either the disciple is apathetic or the discipler desires control and is unwilling to release the learner into ministry.

We see this problem repeatedly in the church in North America. Dependent character is first manifested as dependence on the church structure and leaders, and is rampant across the ecclesiastical spectrum. There is a class structure: clergy and laity. The people look to the church for nurture and instruction rather than to the Bible and the Holy Spirit. They look to pastors and priests for interpretation of Scripture and even for forgiveness. Many Christians reason, "They know what they're talking about and I don't" or "They are in a position closer to God than I." This is dependence. Actually, God gives wisdom to each through the Bible by His Holy Spirit. God has given us many wonderful leaders whose job is to point us to Jesus and help us grow, the goal being spiritual maturity, unity, and increasing dependence on God in every area of life.

People can also tend to look to the church for guidance and direction, even in details. I know of a church where the people feel they must go to their leaders for direction even on questions like, "Should I buy a refrigerator?" This is dependence. The church leadership should help the people look to Jesus, be dependent on Him for guidance and direction and decide for themselves what to buy and when to buy it.

As people drift from personal love relationship with God, however, they *want* this dependence and even become angry if their pastor doesn't give them guidance. This dependence is an easier life than seeking God for oneself, especially if our "first love" has been left. Leaders can begin to see their job as controlling people for their own good, going beyond protection, service and training. The result becomes a struggle when the people's character demands a "king" yet they want freedom and end up resenting the control.

ECCLESIASTICAL STRUCTURES

There are three basic forms of church government. Each form has it own set of advantages and disadvantages. Though the three forms work differently, all three forms have been raised up by God, so we cannot say that one is intrinsically better than the others. The factor that makes all three forms work well is the character of the people (I Sam. 12:14-15). In our analysis, let us assume that everyone is looking to the Lord for wisdom and is trying to come up with His highest. Each form was prevalent in one area of the original 13 American colonies and each is used today by various Christian denominations.

Prevalent in the northern American colonies was the Congregational form of church government. This is essentially a democratic arrangement where the whole congregation gathers together to discuss and vote on the issues as needed. This was the essence of the Mayflower Compact. The people agree to abide by the decision of the majority. Each has input in the deliberation and "owns" the decision personally due to his own participation. It requires the attendance and attention of all.

Prevalent in the southern colonies was the Episcopal form of church government, which is an ecclesiastical monarchy. This was the form in the Jamestown colony imported from England with the Puritans. The pastor is the head of the church and ultimately is responsible for all the decisions. He has advisors and listens to the wisdom of the people. If he makes a bad decision, he will certainly hear from them. Though requiring vigilance, it does not require as much participation. The decision process is much streamlined with this form of church government.

Prevalent in the middle colonies was the Presbyterian form of church government. This is a representative form of government where the people select/elect representatives to do the decision-making. These representatives gather as needed to deliberate among themselves and decide on the issues and policies. The people agree to submit to the decisions of their representatives, and can perhaps remove them if they are not doing well. This involves some participation by the congregation, but not on every detail.

All three forms can work well if the people, lay and leaders alike, are interested in the most godly, Biblical, intelligent solutions to the problems at hand. In all three forms of church government, pride, greed, unbelief, selfishness, apathy and other character failures will diminish effectiveness and quality of governance.

One can imagine the difference in how these three forms work by proposing a hypothetical question to each church, such as "Can a stranded youth group use the church van tomorrow morning for three weeks to continue their evangelistic outreach trip?" The decision would be made in a different manner in each of the three churches.

Abraham Lincoln is reputed to have said that the quality of government in the civil sphere in the next generation follows the quality of government in the ecclesiastical sphere in this generation. And we can see that the quality of government in the ecclesiastical sphere follows the quality of government in the family. The character built in the family will be the character of the church and finally define the quality of the state. We must see revival in America for liberty to be sustained. Then we must understand the specific application of Biblical principles to the sphere of civil government.

CHAPTER XI.

THE AMERICAN EXPERIMENT

Civil government exists to protect rights God has given men.

SPHERE IV. CIVIL GOVERNMENT

When I lecture to Americans, I like to begin this section with a quick, two-question civics test.

The first question is this: "What <u>form</u> of civil government do we have in the United States of America?" Most in the room call out "Democracy!" to which I respond, "No, America is a republic. In fact the founding fathers did everything they could to prevent us from becoming a democracy." As the people in the room begin looking at each other I spring the second question: "We elect representatives to Washington. Their proper job is to vote on the issues the way the people back home want them to vote. True or false?" Usually, most people answer "True." Actually, the answer is "False." Our representatives are not supposed to vote the way they perceive the people want, but they are to vote for what is right and the highest good. We do not delegate our vote to them but we delegate to them the civil government. America is not a representative democracy but a republic. The question immediately arises, "Well, how can anyone stay in office then?" A very good question.

A woman from Hawaii said to me once, "We are accustomed to being a kingdom, but now Hawaii is a republic. But no one knows what that is!"

In a current civics textbook written for Christian schools by a Christian publisher, the definition of the term "republic" was simply,

"A republic is a representative democracy." It went no further.

That we in this country, in which political sovereignty rests in the individual under God rather than the state, do not know what form of government we have, what differentiates a republic from a democracy, or what our representatives are supposed to be doing is a predicament of mammoth proportions.

As background we can go back and consider our two basic presuppositions, that the God of the Bible exists or that He does not exist. From there we can look at the Sovereignty Grid to see who or what is in control. We will omit for this discussion the anarchy side of the Sovereignty Grid since anarchy is only transitional in nature before tyranny.

If an individual believes that God does not exist and that therefore the state is sovereign and has ultimate authority, then he will come to certain conclusions about various issues, and make decisions based on those conclusions.

The idea that the state is sovereign is the basic socialist view of man and the state. Adding the suffix '-ism' to a concept gives that concept an absolute connotation, e.g. materialism or atheism. Simply put, socialism is the notion that the state is the absolute and is ultimately sovereign. Socialism has various political and economic expressions.

The primary function of the socialist state is to control the people externally. The various means the state has to accomplish this include the police force, educational training, psychological manipulation and media indoctrination. The direction of this control comes from the individuals who happen to be in authority in these different areas. The assumption is that the people are dependent on someone to control them. This is tyranny. The option that God can control the individual does not exist because God does not exist in this view. This government relies on external force to control the people.

On the other hand, the Biblical worldview is that God exists and is sovereign. It is the individual's job to control his own life. The direction of this control comes from the law of God, the golden rule, the Bible. The state is to serve the individual with protection and leaves the individual free. This is liberty. This kind of society relies on internal government to control the people.

Let's look at a few specific issues, applying these basic principles to consider the difference between the Christian republic that America started out as and the socialist democracy that we are devolving towards. We will address some basic issues of character, thinking and legal structure

RIGHTS

The socialist view is that the state is sovereign. The state can therefore bestow what rights it wishes concerning its citizens' lives, liberty and property. Since no God has defined these rights, it is the individuals in power who make these decisions. No one is safe. Since the state is sovereign, its pronouncements are by definition good and right. And as the state can give the people rights, the state can take away their rights. So conceivably, the state could bestow special rights of protection on violent or perverse minorities. It could take away the right to life of the most innocent and helpless of its citizens. Or the liberty of political dissenters. Or the property of everyone.

The Bible shows us, however, that God exists and is sovereign. He created the heavens and the earth and man. Having been made in the image of God, men have some specific rights simply by virtue of their existence. These rights are sacred; they cannot be arbitrarily taken away by men. Since God gave life to the individual, included with that life is the right to keep it. Men (individuals, governments, doctors, family) may not take that life away except under narrow, specific conditions given by God the creator. These conditions are outlined earlier.

God created the individual free. That freedom is not unbridled, but includes the corresponding responsibility to govern oneself under God, thus ensuring the highest good. Men may not arbitrarily take that liberty away.

As God created the individual with the ability to choose and create within his context of resources, He gave him rights to property; to own, utilize and dispose of as he wishes. "Property" includes possessions, ideas and especially conscience. Much of the Bible is about owning, maintaining and responsible use of property. Men may not arbitrarily take this property away, neither the state on the one hand (tyranny) nor individuals on the other (anarchy).

These rights are called "natural rights." They are given by God by virtue of the nature of our existence having been created by God and in His image.

History reveals that the strong or loud tend to usurp the rights to life, liberty and property of the weak or shy, both individually and corporately, and capitalize on the labors of others. The purpose of civil government is specifically to protect these natural rights of the people thereby securing their "safety and happiness" and allowing them to be productive. People must design the civil structure to accomplish this purpose. The less these rights are protected in a nation, the more fearful, chaotic and impoverished the nation will be. We see this throughout the world.

James Madison said, "Conscience is the most sacred of all property."[17] The state must not force the individual to do wrong or keep him by force from doing right. This would be a usurpation of his right to his property. It must be noted, however, that "conscience" is not a relative term. It is not individual preference, opinion or feelings, but is measured by God's dictates, laws and desires in the Bible. If a person "feels" that his conscience approves of homosexuality, abortion, child molesting, rape, stealing or murder, it is his conscience that is seared and wrong. If a person feels his conscience cannot allow an abortion provider to continue to live, it is his conscience that is wrong. Conscience is not defined by whatever men feel is "right for them" but by what God requires, regardless of what men may desire. The Bible and God's Law are the measuring rod of conscience.

CONSTITUTION

The American constitution is the design that the founding generation gave to the American civil structure. It is the law by which the state must abide. Noah Webster said, "In free states, the constitution is paramount to the statutes and laws enacted by the legislature, limiting and controlling its power; and in the United States, the legislature is created, and its powers designated, by the constitution."[18] Webster taught Biblical principles of civil government at the constitutional convention. It was he who first standardized the

132

American language and spent almost three decades compiling his 1828 dictionary. It was a Christian dictionary based on the Biblical view of government that God is sovereign.

The purpose of our constitution is to protect the natural rights of the individual, leaving the people free and binding the state under law, dictating how the state should perform its Biblical function of encouraging good and punishing evil. At this point let's look at a few basic misunderstandings about the Constitution.

It is often said today, "I have a constitutional right to own a firearm" or "...to free speech" or "...to an abortion." But actually the Constitution does not give anyone any rights. Rather, God has given certain rights. The Constitution protects those rights from encroachment by the state. The framers of the Constitution were intending to guard against the excessive state control they had suffered under King George. They were intending to slow the damage the state could do when they set up three branches of government to check and balance each other. They specified how the natural rights of the people were to be protected from state interference when they added the Bill of Rights, the first ten amendments.

Since God has given us these rights, included in them are certain responsibilities outlined in the Bible. God has given us the right to property that includes the right to protect it, from the state if necessary. For this reason, the second amendment protects our firearms, a means of protecting our property, from arbitrary seizure by the state. But owning a gun is not a "constitutional right." Responsible use of a gun is implied in gun ownership and the state does have the job of protecting its citizens from ungoverned individuals with guns.

God has given us the right to exercise our liberty, which includes being able to discuss and disseminate our political ideas free from fear of retaliation from the state. The first amendment protects this right to free speech:

> "Congress shall make no law ... abridging the freedom of speech, or of the press..."

But God has not given us the right to say anything we want. He has not given us a right to yell "Fire!" in a crowded theater. This amendment protects the press as a check and balance to civil government, and prohibits the state from shutting it down. God has not, however, given us the right to produce pornography, for instance. God says quite the opposite. This is not a right given by God and therefore is not validly protected by the Constitution. The government's job is to censure evil and encourage good (Rom. 13). The movie rating system is a weak attempt at this. Today, rap singers and others yell "Censorship!! I have a constitutional right to free speech to put out anything I want on a recording for consumption by children!" But this is not true. God has given no right to this activity. It is motivated by greed. The evil needs to be stopped, the good encouraged. This applies also to the "art" sponsored by the National Endowment for the Arts. Somehow, today, showing pornography in the public schools is protected but posting the Ten Commandments or having a Bible study is not. This is the opposite of our God-given right to liberty and makes a sham out of the constitution.

Nowhere has God given us the right to kill our unborn children. Therefore the Constitution does not protect this fictitious right. Laws that limit abortion are not unconstitutional. The right to an abortion is merely a state-granted right.

It has also been said by some that we need a constitutional amendment to ban burning the flag of the United States. But the constitution is a set of limitations on the state, not the people. Legislation to ban flag burning belongs in the body of law, not in the constitution. An amendment to the constitution would define whether the national or state governments could make such a law concerning flag burning.

In summary, we do not have "constitutional rights" bestowed by the state, but "natural rights" given by God and protected by the Constitution. If the state grants rights that protect activities that are against God's law, these rights should be repealed.

DUTY TO ALTER OR ABOLISH

Again, the purpose of a civil government is to protect the natural rights of its citizens. The American Declaration of Independence says that when any government becomes destructive of these ends, it is the right and duty of the people to "alter or abolish" it.

In other words, since the people must set up the state to operate within its God-ordained limits and purposes, when the state supersedes these limits or does not accomplish them, the people must fix the problem.

For us at this time, there is no need to abolish the civil government, but we do need to alter it by replacing our representatives with individuals of tested Christian character and worldview who understand that service and liberty are the ends of government and not control. Their job is to keep laws within their proper boundaries, thereby governing the government.

CONTROL OR PROTECTION?

Referring to the Sovereignty Grid, under the philosophy of government that the State is sovereign, there is a political spectrum of various forms of civil government. On the left is International Socialism - communism. On the right is National Socialism - Naziism, fascism, and other right-wing dictatorships.

In the center is Democratic Socialism or Socialist Democracy. This is where the people have a voice through their vote but the majority rules; the state is sovereign having been elected by the majority.

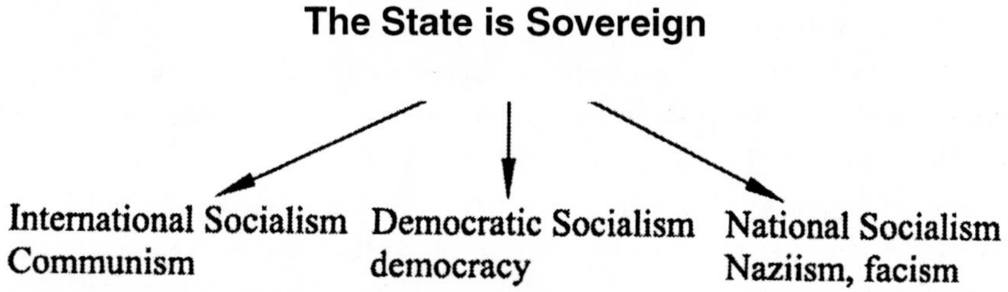

The State is Sovereign

International Socialism   Democratic Socialism   National Socialism
Communism   democracy   Naziism, facism

Fig. 11.1 Socialist Political Spectrum.

While these different governments vary in form and operation, they are all based on the same presupposition. They are not really alternatives to each other but merely differ on the means to the same end - control.

In the Biblical view, the structure of the state would be set up by the people to secure the God-given unalienable natural rights of its citizens, and protect them from those who are not self-governed. Political sovereignty rests in the individual under God and he chooses (in effect, hires) representatives to perform the proper functions of governing.

The American constitution is the first document in the history of the world to establish a national form of Christian self-government, uniting a group of states under a national government, and then be *agreed upon by the people.*

The American Constitution combined into a representative civil government the three forms of church government prevalent in the colonies at the time. These were the congregational form of church government, the episcopal form of church government, and the presbyterian form of church government. That representatives, believing deeply in these diverse ideas, got together and hammered out this combination into a national government that actually protects liberty is evidence of the hand of God in history. There were the Congregationalists who were afraid of tyranny, the Episcopals who were afraid of anarchy, and the Presbyterians who were afraid of both. The result was a Christian Federal Constitutional Republic. It took two years to be ratified by the people. It embodied the Biblical principles of civil government. The state is the servant of the individual. Our representatives are called "public servants."

This is why America is truly an experiment. Its foundation is the character of the people, not an external structure of force. As we decline in character internally, we shift externally from a Christian republic to a socialist representative democracy, as in Fig. 11.2. Socialism begins in the heart as the individual shifts in dependence from God to man.

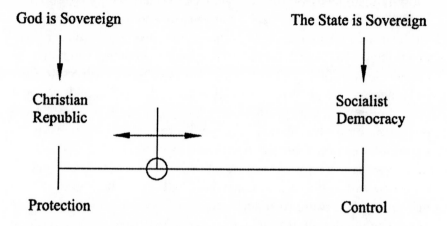

Fig. 11.2 Christian Republic Or Socialist Democracy?

Generally in the U.S., both republicans and democrats are socialists in their philosophy of government. Even Christians in the U.S. are generally socialist in their thinking.

It might be pointed out that the United States is a "Christian nation" only with respect to the Biblical principles on which it was founded, not on the basis of how many of its citizens are Christians or how righteous the decisions of the political leaders are. In these latter respects, we are in decline.

ELECTIONS

What are we doing when we go to the polls and vote? Our presuppositions will define our mentality concerning our representatives.

In a socialist democracy we are electing a ruler to rule us. His method of making decisions is to tally the calls from back home and cast his vote in accordance with the perceived majority. Minorities get trampled this way, but if the state is sovereign, who is to say that's bad? Apathetic majorities get trampled in this way also.

In a Christian republic we are governing ourselves in the civil sphere through representatives we elect. In effect we are hiring individuals to govern, making their decisions based on righteousness and the common good. They work for us in this sphere, so we must communicate to them not just what we think but why we think it. These individuals should be the most Godly and intelligent people in the land with a Biblical, not a socialist, philosophy of civil government. They will come up against some knotty problems and will need to know how to find real answers, and not just make answers up.

Since we are governing ourselves, we <u>must</u> vote, and we must vote intelligently. One problem with liberty is that it produces prosperity and ease, then apathy. If we will not govern ourselves in the sphere of the state, then others will rule over us.

I was in a pastor's meeting shortly before a recent election where a Bible-believing Christian had been defeated in the primaries. The topic of discussion was "Now whom do we vote for?" The general discouragement was stated by one of the pastors, "It's just the lesser of two evils."

We have all heard people say something like, "It's just the lesser of two evils. I'm not even going to vote." But this is an error for Christians. Apathy is one manifestation of a lack of Christian character.

We must always vote for the lesser of two evils. There are at least two reasons why. First, if we do not vote for the lesser of two evils then we may get the greater of two evils. Secondly, we will never have any other choice, because Jesus is not running for office! Not only must we vote for this individual but also we must work for his election. This takes time and energy.

PRINCIPLE: Elections are about character, not economics.

If our representative is supposed to vote for what is right and the highest good, it will require a Biblical, literate populace who understand righteousness and who *want* the common good to elect him into office. A people who desire those in office who return to them the most personal benefit will not elect him.

We must remember that every time a representative votes, he is voting his conscience, whether his conscience tells him that the right choice is the good of the people in light of the merits of the law, his perception of the people's wishes or his desire to remain in office through the votes his largesse will gain him. This is why elections are about character, not economics.

GEORGE WASHINGTON KING?

In the Erie, Pennsylvania airport, a copy of a letter written by George Washington to one of his officers concerning an offer to make him king of the new nation was displayed. The caption beneath it read as follows:

This reply to Colonel Louis Nicola, written May 22, 1782 sharply rebukes the colonel for his letter suggesting a coup d'etat to make Washington king. Nicola, one of the oldest, wisest and most dignified of Washington's commanders had boldly put in writing what was secretly discussed in all ranks of the recently victorious American army. Officers and men alike, thoroughly dissatisfied and disgusted with their treatment by congress, were ripe for such a plot. Had the commander-in-chief been susceptible to the blandishments of friends like Nicola, his tremendous popularity, both within the army and without, probably would have assured a successful revolt and the establishment of a monarchy. Never did the greatness of Washington's character shine more brightly than in this repudiation of the idea. The original letter reproduced here is in the library of congress.

Sir:

With a mixture of great surprise and astonishment I have read with attention the Sentiments you have submitted to my perusal. Be assured, Sir, no occurrence in the course of the War has given me more painful sensations than your information of their being such ideas existing in the Army as you have expressed, and I must view with abhorrence, and reprehend with severity. For the present, the communication of them will rest in my own bosom, unless some further agitation of the matter shall make a disclosure necessary.

I am much at a loss to conceive what part of my conduct could have given encouragement to an address which to me seems big with the greatest mischiefs that can befall my Country. If I'm not deceived in the knowledge of myself, you could not have found a person to whom your schemes are more disagreeable; at the same time, in justice to my own feelings I must add, that no Man possesses a more sincere wish to see ample justice done to the

Army than I do, and as far as my powers and influence, in a constitutional way extend, they shall be employed to the utmost of my abilities to effect it, should there be any occasion. Let me conjure you then, if you have any regard for your Country, concern for yourself or your posterity, or respect for me, to banish these thoughts from your Mind and never communicate, as from yourself, or anyone else, a sentiment of the like Nature.

  With esteem, I am your most obedient servant,
      George Washington[19]

  Here, Washington is an example of the Christian character needed in the people we elect to public office, character desiring the highest good, even at personal expense, and able to resist the great temptation of power.

LAW

  Where does law come from? If we believe God does not exist, then law did not come from Him, obviously. So men make up the laws. There are no moral absolutes. There is no right and wrong. Men generate laws to fit the situation. We look around us to get a consensus of what is, look at history perhaps to see what has been, and vote on what ought to be. The wife of a U.S. Vice-President said a few years back, "We should legalize marijuana because so many people are doing it." That question has come up again recently. What about rape? Potentially, literally any evil thing could become legal (murdering babies?), and any good thing could become illegal (Christian education?) if the state is sovereign.

  In a Christian republic, the modifier "Christian" denotes the recognition that God is sovereign and has given law, and that right and wrong do exist. Civil law, then, must not be inconsistent with God's law. The Bible says that man's law must encourage good and discourage evil (Rom. 13:1-4). Law is based on absolutes.

  All men are equal under God's law, so they should be equal under man's law, male or female, rich or poor, black or white. Laws that are partial to one group over another are wrong. Laws that benefit one group at the expense of another are wrong. Wrong laws should be altered.

CENTRALIZATION

The essence of the American political system is limited government.

In a socialist democracy, the state is sovereign and exists to control the people, so anything that increases the power of the state is good and anything that works against the state is evil. The actions of the state try to centralize power, thereby giving the ability for more control, "for the good of the people." In the extreme this includes measures like executing people for dissent.

By contrast, in a Christian republic the actions of the state try to keep power decentralized in the hands of the people themselves.

Again, the people's character defines how this works. A few years back, the U.S. president had a plan to decentralize welfare from the national government to the states. This was an opportunity to increase local control and therefore quality, and reap great financial savings as well. The states rejected it, not wanting to take on the responsibility, so that power ultimately did not get shifted down and decentralized.

Actually, helping the poor is the job of the church, but because the church has ceased to take it on, authority over this area has shifted upwards to the state. Author and Bible scholar George Grant points out that historically, the Christian family has been the primary agent of care for the poor and afflicted. He shows that if, in America, each Christian family took care of its own poor, and each church took care of its own poor, and then each church took on *one* welfare case additionally, the national welfare dole would be entirely eliminated.[20] This solution would provide far better care with more effective use of recourses. Economically, this would help these impoverished people become productive and non-dependent again, not only saving hundreds of billions of tax dollars, but increasing tax revenues from their productivity. Not to mention influencing them towards Christ instead of the state.

Another problem with centralized power is that as the state becomes more powerful, the possibility and reality of corruption on the part of those in office increases. To work for centralized government is to work for increased corruption. We cannot decry corruption while working for more powerful civil government.

EDUCATION

In a socialist democracy, since the state is sovereign, the purpose of education is to solidify state power by creating in the people a socialist character of dependence on the state. The goal of education here is to aggrandize the state.

In a Christian republic the purpose of education is to create individual self-governing Christian character and dependence on God, and personal independence from the state. The goal is to keep the state in its proper place, fulfilling its proper functions. The goal is not to eliminate the state; that is the anarchist's goal.

In the extreme, the socialist state viewing itself as sovereign claims that the people, their energies, their property and even their children belong to it. Education, therefore, is the job of the state, even if it needs to go around the parents. The Bible says, however, that God has given children to parents and has made education the job of the parents. The state is accountable to the people to accomplish certain functions, education not among them. Parents may delegate this function to someone else, but must not abdicate this responsibility.

In some places in the United States, this difference in views has been contested over the question of home schooling. Should parents be required to notify the local school board that they are home schooling their children, or should they be required to get the school board's consent in order to home school their children? Notification or consent? Are children the property and responsibility of their parents or of the state? Is the job of the state to protect and serve, or to control? Will we fight for liberty or submit to tyranny?

MORALITY

Again, in the socialist state the rulers are active in the individual's life because the state depends on external government to control the people. In a Christian republic, the leaders are restrained in the lives of the people because it depends on internal government, i.e. the people controlling themselves under God. This decentralization of power produces liberty. This is why we need a great spiritual awakening.

If one doesn't believe that God exists, or know Him personally, he can't really see an alternative to external control. "Unless you are born again, you cannot see the kingdom of God" (John 3:3). The less internal control in a society, the greater the call (and need) for external control. So in a perverse way, a decline in morality is in the interest of the state, shifting power upward to those individuals in office. The ruler can become more powerful by encouraging a decline in morality. Those who reject morality play right into his hands and never know how they have been used...and they are the ones who suffer the consequences of their immorality while those in power reap the political benefit.

This decline must be reversed. We as individuals must get to know God through Jesus Christ, and reform our own personal lives in every area in accordance with the Bible and the ways of God. This is revival.

Americans are generally unwilling to believe their fellow countrymen would stoop to such manipulative means. We know, however, that men are sinful and history shows that they are disposed to use whatever opportunity arises for personal gain at the expense of others. This is a significant lesson of history.

When the Constitution was finally signed in Philadelphia by the representatives of the states, accounts say that a hush came over the founding fathers. They realized that though this written constitution secured the liberties of the people on paper, there was no basis for this government but the character of the people.

Could it last?

As they came out of the hall, a lady reportedly asked Benjamin Franklin, "What kind of government have you given us?" He responded, "A republic, if you can keep it!"

Ultimately we will get the civil government that we deserve, one that reflects the character of the people.

LEADERSHIP

What makes a strong leader?

In a socialist democracy the strong leader is the demagogue. He persuades by emotion and charisma, swaying the unthinking masses by promises of personal peace and prosperity. If the masses are indeed unthinking and their primary concern is their own personal peace and prosperity, he will prevail.

This means that a decline in literacy shifts a nation towards socialism and is therefore in the interest of the state, as is a decline in morality. We are seeing this decline in the United States.

In a Christian republic, the leader persuades by principle, promising righteousness and the highest good. The populace, then, must understand principle and be able to figure out what the highest good is in order for this person to be elected. They must want the highest good. They must be able to be reasoned with, not just be swayed by emotion.

In a Christian republic, the leader is a servant not a ruler. He must be self-governed to resist amassing wealth and power to himself. He has the power to spend the people's money on himself and buy votes, and the power to borrow unlimited amounts of money that he will not have to repay, but future taxpayers will. So those we elect must be the Godliest people with the greatest integrity. Elections are about character, not economics. It is amazing that congressmen can vote themselves huge pay increases in times of financial crisis and still be re-elected to office. But then the character of the people defines the character of the representatives they elect. As long as we are dependent in character, we vote for the candidates who will apparently meet our need, no matter what they do.

TAXES

In a socialist democracy a tax increase is seen as good. This centralizes power, removing economic power from the individual and transferring it to the state. To buy votes, the rulers use taxes to increase their power and strengthen their hold on office through various programs, entitlements and pork projects. Entitlements are funds that certain people are "entitled to" due to different circumstances: poverty, having children out of wedlock, low income, age, minority status, etc. I heard a congressman say on the radio, "We would incorporate these deductions into the tax code, but it would cost the government billions of dollars." This statement assumes that the government owns all money and allows the people to keep some of it. The state letting you keep some of your money is seen as benevolence. Actually, you own your money and pay some of it to the state to enable it to fund its programs. Proper taxation requires vigilant oversight.

In a Christian republic the goal is to decrease taxes. This decentralizes economic power and leaves it in the hands of the individual. There was no national income tax in the U. S. before 1913. My own grandfather remembers the promise, "It will never get above two percent." For the previous 120 years the national government had run without income taxes. Getting back to that situation will entail a major disruption.

In the 1980's, as taxes were decreased in the U. S., the economy boomed; when taxes began to be increased the economy stalled, actually decreasing tax revenues. The constitution authorizes the congress to pass laws for the "general welfare." The term "general welfare" is meant to restrict congress to legislation that benefits the entire nation collectively. The congress is not authorized to pass laws and spending programs that benefit only particular states, communities, individuals, industries, ethnic groups, economic classes or other special interests. These are local welfare, not general welfare. Half the federal budget consists of direct benefit payments to individuals, i.e. entitlements. In addition there is spending on local community projects, such as $2.5 million for a parking garage in Iowa. Taxpayers throughout the country are paying for projects like that.

SEPARATION OF POWERS

If we believe the state is sovereign, that which slows down the process of the state is seen as evil, impeding control. The governing mentality is activism.

Executive activism, legislative activism and judicial activism all centralize power in the national government. The Supreme Court was never meant to generate law, using its own previous decisions as precedents equal to law. It was intended to check whether the actions of congress were constitutional. Congress was to generate law.

Executive-branch bureaucrats were not meant to generate law either. They are unelected. School districts are going bankrupt because of "unfunded mandates" from government agencies for unnecessary or undesired educational programs. Unfunded mandates are various programs mandated by government agencies or congress without corresponding financial allocation. This is control, not protection. In California, the national government is requiring the state to pay, with state funds, for full health and welfare benefits for illegal aliens flooding in from Mexico and Central America.

A Christian republic recognizes that God is sovereign and that the state exists to protect the individual. Since God is sovereign, no man or group of men is sovereign. The powers of government, executive, legislative and judicial are therefore separated so that they check and balance each other and to impede control and keep the state in its proper place. Isaiah tells us,

> "For the Lord is our judge,
> The Lord is our lawgiver,
> The Lord is our king;
> He will save us." Is. 33:22

The three functions of government are safe together in an all-loving God, but are not safe in the hands of fallen men. The true greedy nature of men is taken into account and the powers check each other to keep individuals from running away with the civil government. The governing mentality is restraint, allowing the people to govern their own lives while protecting their liberties. People need more freedom not less, with protection. A two-party system is another valuable check that keeps both parties honest. The press is another valuable check and balance.

An ominous election motto recently was "Re-invent government." This meant to change from a restrained government to an active government. The people are saying, "Why isn't the government doing something for me?" Fixing the economy, the schools, the cities, the youth? When the character of the people wants the state to be active, there are plenty of people who would be glad to oblige. The party running on restraint at this point will lose elections. The people will lose their freedom.

For example, education is not ultimately the responsibility of civil government but of parents, but as the character of the people says, "Why doesn't the state educate my children for me, for free?" a public education system arises to do the job.

JURISDICTION

Jurisdiction refers to the extent or range of authority to govern, and is defined in the Tenth Amendment. The division of power between the national and state government is another check and balance. The amendment states:

> "The powers not delegated to the United States by the Constitution, nor prohibited by it to the states, are reserved to the states respectively, or to the people."

This amendment limits the powers of the national government to those specifically enumerated in the Constitution. As we look at the issues and national control of various aspects of our lives, whether health care, education, individual welfare or entitlement programs, we must ask ourselves some questions, "Civil government has a specific job; is this area part of that job? Does the national government have any business at all in this area? If not, whose job is it? Is this control or protection? Is this a move towards tyranny or liberty? How has this area come to have been taken over by the civil government?"

It has been said that eternal vigilance is the price of liberty. If we are not vigilant, our liberty will evaporate.

CHURCH AND STATE

The goal in a socialist democracy is to exclude religion from the affairs of state altogether. The thinking goes, "If God does not exist, what role does myth have in running a nation?" As long as Christians keep their faith in the devotional compartment of their lives and do not influence the actions of the state, they can be tolerated. Through history, however, refusal to do this has led to martyrdom. Liberal Christianity is acceptable to the state because, built on the same presuppositions, it doesn't impede the state. Bible-believing Christianity is not acceptable because it calls the state into account.

In a Christian republic, the goal is to protect the church from encroachment by the state, and to protect the individual from the abuses of a state/church alliance. The individual's freedom to apply God's truth to every area of life, unobstructed by the state or a state church, is to be protected.

The establishment clause of the first amendment is only one sentence long:

> "Congress shall make no law respecting an establishment of religion, or prohibiting the free exercise thereof."

The intent was to protect the church from the state, not vice versa. The founder's intent was not to disassociate the state from its Biblical foundations.

THE RIGHT TO LIFE

If we believe God does not exist and that we evolved by chance, then who defines the term "life"? Should every individual define life for himself? Should doctors, politicians, educators, scientists or some other elite? Maybe the majority? At any rate, men define the term "life," and it therefore becomes a relative term. It can be redefined as needed. Our definition may be extended to include whether a life is "wanted" life or "meaningful" life. Our definition may be that life begins at conception, or three months after conception, or at natural birth. Or perhaps, as some are suggesting, three months after natural birth. If at that time the fetus is meaningful, healthy, the right gender, wanted, and matches whatever other criteria we want, the blob of tissue can be granted the status "alive" by the state, become a person and come under constitutional protection. Otherwise it can be eliminated like a liver or a tumor.

At the other end of life, if some elite, or the majority, decides that a person's life is not "meaningful life" due to poor health and/or advanced age, political views or even race as in Nazi Germany, then life can be defined as having ended.

But God is sovereign and, having created human life, it is He, not man, who is in charge of when it begins and ends. Each person has a natural right to his life that cannot be taken away and must be protected by the state. The term "life" is an absolute term and the state must work within that framework.

The existence of abortion and euthanasia requires action. However, action must be thought-through, prayed-through Biblical action, not anarchy.

The way to help babies is:

1) Help the moms. Christians should be saying, "I will help you. My church will help you. I'll house you. I'll pay for the baby. I'll pay for the doctor. I'll pay for adoption. I'll give you a job. I'll teach you to be a good parent. I'll buy clothes for you. I'll pay for your education. I'll help you!" This is Christian self-government in action.

2) Spend our time and energy getting Godly Christians into political office at every level. Not "Christian socialists" but Biblical, intelligent, loving, self-governing servants. This is a long-term solution and takes continuous vigilance, not just a one-shot splash. Their job includes protecting the lives of children not yet born.

NATIONAL SOVEREIGNTY

There is a continual call for a unified global governing structure. There has always been someone who has desired and/or tried to rule the world. This is the end result of pride. Lucifer decided he would "make [himself] like the most high" (Is. 14:14) and rule the universe. But God is opposed to the proud and gives grace to the humble; the meek will inherit the earth (James 4:6, Matt. 5:5).

In 1977, Norman Cousins, editor of Saturday Review, said in a meeting at the University of Illinois that the "creation of a rational world order should be the keystone of American foreign policy." He stressed the "urgency of ceding national sovereignty to limited world governance over problems boundaries can't contain."[21] This one-world government has been preached for a long time as the solution to our problems. The Humanist Manifesto of 1973 states this:

"...We have reached a turning point in human history where the best option is to transcend the limits of national sovereignty and to move toward the building of world community... Thus we look to the development of a system of world law and world order based upon transnational federal government."[22]

The Bible says that the Antichrist will be at the top of any global political empire, and will rule with violence and terror. This is the ultimate centralization and the occasion for the ultimate corruption.

The phrase "transcend national sovereignty" assumes that global government is "transcendent" or better than national sovereignty. We see this centralization being attempted in Europe and in North America at the same time as the world's tyrannical empires are breaking up. At the same time, nationalism, or making one's own nation the absolute, is not the answer either, whether in America, Germany or Russia.

We should ask ourselves, "Can civil government control sin?" As we have watched the violence in the freed communist nations of Eastern Europe, we see that freedom does not guarantee that things will go well. When Communism fell in Yugoslavia, along with freedom came a resurfacing of ethnic hatreds and violence that precipitated war and then occupation by the United Nations. While external government can restrain the violence, it is the internal government, the character of the people, that will allow freedom to continue. The ultimate answer is not in the sword, but in Jesus and His word, the Bible.

THE SOLUTION

Jesus told us, "All authority has been given to Me in heaven and earth. Go therefore and make disciples of all the nations, baptizing them in the name of the Father and the Son and the Holy Spirit, teaching them to observe all that I commanded you; and lo, I am with you always, even to the end of the age," (Matt. 28:18-19). The solution to the world's problems is the Gospel of Jesus Christ.

CHAPTER XII.

ECONOMICS

The creation of prosperity.

It is said that economics is the tenant in the house of civil government.

In 1776, in the same year that a civil form of Christian self-government began to emerge in the American Declaration of Independence, a book on the nature of Christian self-government and economics, Wealth of Nations, was published by Adam Smith in England. Its premise was that if two people are left free from government interference to decide on a transaction, both will go away satisfied. On a larger scale, if the market is left free from government interference to make economic decisions, then all parties will go away satisfied and will be encouraged to produce and consume more. This combination of civil and economic self-government brought about a powerful historical advance in liberty and prosperity.

This concept is based on the idea that the individual is to govern himself in every area of his life, including economics. The purpose of civil government is to provide protection, not to control, and to leave the individual free to pursue whatever vocation to which he feels called and best suited. He finds a need that someone has and serves him by filling that need, trading his time, labor and ingenuity for an agreed upon equivalent in currency. With this money he can pay others who serve him by providing him with goods and services. They in turn do the same, etc.

The basis of liberty is the character of the people. The basis of a good economy is also the character of the people. Let's look at how an economy works in its most basic terms.

The purpose of an economy is to provide <u>material well being</u> (MWB) for individuals. This material well being includes things like food and drink, clothing and shelter, transportation and communication, health care, education and recreation. Material well being is a good thing; it is safe to say that God wants every people and nation to have a high level of material well being. God is grieved over the starving in India, the homeless in America and the street kids in Brazil.

Materialism, however, is when material things become the absolute, and money and security become the focus and are worshiped and served. This is not good. In fact, Jesus said that you cannot serve both God and money (Matt 6:24).

A related question is whether there is a wrong level of material well being. Are riches wrong?

The Bible says not that *money* is the root of evil, but that *the love of money* is the root of all kinds of evil (I Tim. 6:10). So the problem is not a level of MWB, but an attitude about MWB. At any level of MWB, rich or poor, if we trust in riches rather than God or put MWB before God, then it becomes wrong. At the same time, the Bible also tells us what to do with riches and warns us of their distracting power.

Since we are to love our neighbor and ourselves, we want to increase material well being. Economic expansion is good; living for money is not. The Bible tells us this in Deuteronomy:

> "But you shall remember the Lord your God, for it is He who is giving you power to make wealth, that He may confirm His covenant which He swore to your fathers, as it is this day.
> "And it shall come about if you ever forget the Lord your God, and go after other gods and serve them and worship them, I testify against you today that you shall surely perish. " Deut. 8:18-19

THE SOURCE OF MATERIAL WELL-BEING[23]

PRINCIPLE - The blessing of a good economy is the ability to buy the necessities of life with fewer man-hours of labor.

The "ability to buy" means not being dependent on others economically. "Fewer man-hours" means more money left over to support the church and charity, support world missions and help the poor. It also means more free time available to worship God and serve others, to increase education and to enjoy recreation, which factors in turn increase productivity.

If there is lack of character, however, money and free time are spent on dissipation, excess consumption and lusts. This in turn *decreases* productivity, decreasing MWB, and decreasing liberty.

We will use a basic formula to represent how MWB is produced:

$$NR + (HE \times T) = MWB$$
Natural resources + (Human Energy multiplied by Tools) = MWB

In this formula NR represents the natural resources available. We said earlier that a nation is only individual people, in various relationships to each other, on a body of resources. What a people does with these resources (sit on them, use them or waste them) is as important as the presence of the resources.

HE represents human energies, both mental and physical, applied to these resources to develop them.

T represents tools, which are the means of production, that which multiplies the human energy applied to the natural resources to produce material well being. These tools must be invented, which requires ideas and creativity. Then they must be built or invested in, which takes money. Better tools multiply human energy better, increasing productivity and MWB.

In the last century the electric motor multiplied human energy rapidly, beginning the industrial revolution. Various forms of transportation and methods of communication are tools that have vastly multiplied human energy, but have required much time, research and great amounts of capital to produce. The computer has been a great multiplier of human energy in recent years. Better and more numerous tools have brought about increased MWB.

PRINCIPLE: Increased productivity consists in producing

better quality products at increased efficiency.

Better quality products or services are the result of conscientious workmanship and quality tools. The Bible says that we should do everything as unto the Lord. This is the basis for the value of one's work and vocation. The Biblical work ethic says there is value in our labor and production even in the smallest things by virtue of the investment of our time and life. Our production is a reflection of the nature of God as a creative being. So excellence, beauty, organization, utility and service should characterize our work, too. As we have fallen away from God, our basis for craftsmanship and quality has diminished, as personal responsibility has been greatly eroded. Production has become regarded as a necessary evil tolerated for the sake of gain. Individual excellence has been replaced by the "quality control department."

Better products are the result of ideas, innovations and perceptions of the need.

Efficiency is the ability to make more units per man-hour of labor.

As we produce more of these high quality products per man-hour of labor, the cost per unit decreases because there are fewer hours of labor in each.

This produces more sales and larger markets.

This produces more profit.

This produces higher wages and more jobs.

This increases MWB.

This is good!

What things are hindrances to increased production and MWB? Some hindering factors are dishonesty, illiteracy, the television which produces a consumer rather than a producer mentality, hopelessness, dissipation (drugs and alcohol), fear of risk, decreased tools, and a decreased capital pool from increased taxation and government regulation, interest on debt or excess consumption.

On the other hand, production is increased by integrity, education, less television, hope, abstinence, courage, increased tools, savings, hard labor, smart labor, charity and liberty.

All these factors are reflections of with the character level of the society, the education of the people, the inherited circumstances, and the quality of personal relationships in the nation.

The environment for economic freedom is established and protected by civil government. This environment includes protection of property, enforcement of contracts, economic freedom, minimal taxes, encouraging charity, releasing the entrepreneur and a balanced budget without debt.

It is interesting that in many nations where the civil government excessively controls or even obstructs the economy, there are flourishing underground economies that produce a large portion of the goods and services. In those nations where this economic activity is on the sly, enterprise is free but unprotected. It has been suggested that in these nations, if the state would give up the desire to control everything and would release liberty, providing protection to these enterprises, vast economic prosperity would result.[24] Reasonable tax revenues could be levied for infrastructure development. The socialist state exists, however, to control the people, and corruption funnels tax revenues into personal pockets.

Hong Kong was set up as an experiment to see what would happen to an economy with no government interference at all, only protection. It is booming.[25]

I have been in various nations in the world where there has been an economically based anti-American sentiment. In these nations, America is seen as wealthy and therefore unjust. Typically, in these nations economic opportunity is scarce, and the way to become wealthy is by corruption. In America, the way to become wealthy is through conscientious hard work in a context of freedom, serving the needs of others in some way or another. This basic mentality is still widespread and there is still freedom and opportunity, so there is widespread wealth in America. Many of these other nations, however, have only seen wealth as the product of the strong abusing the weak, and they deduce that America must be robbing the rest of the world. Their economic model is socialism.

To have economic expansion and liberty, we must both learn and teach to our children the character needed to increase production (internal government) and the principles they will need to guide them in their choice of representatives to keep the state in its proper role protecting opportunity (external government). We must build for the future and occupy until He comes.

CHAPTER XIII.

EDUCATION FOR LIBERTY

All education produces character.

As God changes a nation, education is a crucial step, and not only that education must take place but also that a particular kind of education must take place. In order to sustain liberty, education must have both content and methodology designed for that purpose.

The Bible tells us that the quality of any society is dependent on the character of the people:

1) Political stability is dependent on individual Christian character. (I Sam. 12:14-16)
2) Economic prosperity is dependent on individual Christian character. (Deut. 8:18-19)
3) Wisdom and understanding are dependent upon individual Christian character. (Prov. 9:9-16)

All education produces character. Character defines liberty. This is the link between education and the quality of society.

Since education is the process of training character, whether at school, at home or at church, we must answer the question, "What kind of character do we want to produce and how do we produce it?"

When inquiring about a school, we typically ask the question, "What curriculum do you use?" If we know what curriculum is used, we have a general idea about the educational program and the kind of students that are turned out.

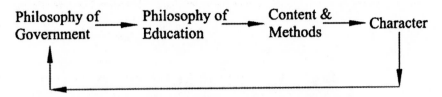

Fig. 13.1 Education And Government

Referring to Figure 13.1, the curriculum consists of a particular content taught by particular methods, "the what and the how" of the education. The content and methods are defined by a philosophy of education that tells us *why* we are teaching what we are teaching in the way we are teaching it.

But there is a preliminary step that defines our philosophy of education, and that is our philosophy of government. Our education and the character it develops will be defined by our view of sovereignty.

PRINCIPLE: Our philosophy of government will define our philosophy of education in such a way that both the content and the methods used will produce a character in the individual that reinforces that philosophy of government.

We can look at our Sovereignty Grid for education below to see how this works.

SOVEREIGNTY GRID — EDUCATION

I. Philosophy of Government -- View of sovereignty

left extreme	Biblical	right extreme
Individual is sovereign. Anarchy. No civil control. No government.	God is sovereign. Liberty with law. Civil government by consent. Internal government.	State is sovereign. Tyranny. Total civil control. External government.

II. Philosophy of Education
No basis in truth (relativism).	Basis -- Bible understanding.	Basis -- Bible detail, doctrine.

No reasoning	Reasoning ability taught	No reasoning -- rote: learn what is given by authority
Public education in America.	American Christian education.	Private education in America, much Christian education.
Illiterate -- can't read or think	Literate -- able to read and reason to valid conclusions.	Illiterate -- able to read but not reason and apply material.
Hates education -- no purpose.	Loves education -- becomes a self-educating student.	Hates education -- rote, detail.
Ignorance.	Education.	Indoctrination.

III. Methods

Draw out child (autonomy). "How do you feel about...?" Implant facts sensorially.	Both pour in then draw out thoughts and conclusions. Facts and memory plus reasoning from facts.	Pour in facts, memory, recitation. Packaged curriculum.
Emphasis – emotions, experience everything.	Emphasis -- will, character, understand why.	Emphasis – mind, know lots of things.
Child is sensory being -- senses, feelings.	Child is governing being -- Bible, reason, concepts.	Child is intellectual being - facts and details.
Workbook approach.	Notebook approach.	Textbook approach.
Psychological testing -- stimulus/response.	Essay testing.	Standardized testing.
No homework.	Homework as needed to master subject.	Keep 'em busy.
Child intensive.	Teacher intensive.	Material intensive.

IV. Character

Ungoverned --therefore dependent.	Internally governed -- independent.	Externally governed, i.e. dependent.
Peer sensitive (fears peers).	God sensitive (fears God).	Authority sensitive (fears authority).
Autonomous character -- rebellion, hedonism.	Self-governed character under God – liberty.	Slave character -- cults, etc.
Can be manipulated due to ignorance.	Cannot be manipulated.	Can be manipulated due to follow-the-leader mentality.
Obeys self -- feels hypocritical choosing against emotions.	Obeys God -- confident choosing right, against either emotions or authority.	Obeys authority (blindly) -- feels guilty choosing against authority.

V. Government

Child (Individual) is King.	God is King.	State (or Church) is King.
Anarchy.	Liberty with law.	Tyranny.
No law freedom but chaos.	Law written on the heart -- order and freedom.	External law order but slavery.

PUBLIC EDUCATION IN AMERICA

The philosophy of government on the left of the Sovereignty Grid for Education sees the individual as sovereign in and of himself. It designs its education to produce what is known as the autonomous or self-actualized child. This 'autonomy' is a major goal of American public Humanist education. This is the child who recognizes no authority higher than self.

Since this view of education presupposes that God does not exist, the Bible should have no place in the school; everyone's religion is equally valid. Therefore, teaching that Jesus is the Savior of the world was removed from the schools in Massachusetts in the 1830's by Horace Mann in an attempt to provide "non-sectarian" education.

This type of education focuses on the emotions and the senses and sees the child as a "sensory being." The idea is that if a person experiences everything, then he is educated. No basis in truth is taught — God doesn't exist so there are no absolutes, no truth. No reasoning is taught because experience is the goal. I was taught in college that "consistency is the hobgoblin of small minds" by professors who were attempting to debunk reason in favor of experience.

This leads to existentialism. I know a man who was once a math professor at the University of Illinois. While lying under a tree one day, he suddenly realized that *he was the tree*! This was quite an experience, which he described as "religious." He realized that the tree was god and that the ground was god and that he was god. This is Hinduism. Soon he was no longer confidant that 2 plus 2 actually equaled 4, so he switched from Mathematics to the College of Education teaching future teachers educational psychology.

Another major goal of this Humanist education is called "group dependence." It is theorized that if the people are highly peer sensitive, then no one will get too far out of line. This is seen as a way to control the people externally — a sort of herd mentality. "Socialization" has superseded academics as the purpose of education. Political Correctness is an example of external control by shame and fear.

In the extreme, this education produces an individual who is illiterate; he cannot read and he cannot reason. As a result he hates education, seeing no purpose in it. He grows to be peer sensitive and unable to think for himself. His self-centered mentality rejects being governed by authorities in his life: parents, teachers, police, God. He is "self-actualized." This leads to hedonism: "if it feels good, do it." He has been focussed on his own emotions as the indicator of reality. On the other hand it leads to rebellion as authorities attempt to control him. This ungoverned person, however, is actually dependent on others for control.

I once tutored a boy who had graduated from fifth grade in a California public school. This boy literally could not read. He did not know what it meant when I told him to "sound out" a word. After laboring through a short paragraph, I asked him a few questions that required a minimum of deduction to apply what we had read. He was blank! Totally. He hated it; he felt picked on. This concerned me because here was a young man of reasonable intelligence who would be dependent on someone else, especially peers or the media, to tell him what to think. He could be manipulated due to ignorance. And he had no idea what was causing his problem.

Discipline under this education is virtually non-existent.

This education reinforces the philosophy of government that the individual is sovereign.

The duty of civil government is to protect the liberty of parents to decide upon the education of their children. It is not to control education. The most powerful social force is the desire of parents for a better life for their children, and opportunity to accomplish that goal should be protected.

CHRISTIAN EDUCATION IN AMERICA

As test scores have dropped in public education since the 1960's, and rebellion has increased, private schools and Christian education have risen to teach basic skills and Biblical moral values again. Parents who recognized these problems in the product of public education began to make a shift in their thinking. Instead of seeing the child as a "sensory being," the pendulum swung to seeing the child as an "intellectual being." The emphasis was now placed on the mind. The thought here came to be that if a person knows a lot of things, then he is educated.

Much of Christian education swung over to the right side of the Sovereignty Grid for Education. This type of Christian education once again includes the Bible, but consists of vast amounts of facts and details in all areas of the curriculum. The Bible is taught in terms of Bible stories, Bible details, and Bible verses, all memorized by rote. The child is tested with matching, short answer, and fill-in-the-blank tests. The student does not read and study the Bible but learns facts about the Bible from another text and fills in blanks in an external workbook. Thus he tends to learn that the Bible is a secondary text, not the primary source of wisdom and life.

Reasoning is still not taught, but the student is expected to memorize and believe what the authority gives him. The student becomes dependent on external authority to know what to think. In the extreme, the mentality is, "The Bible said it. I believe it. That settles it. Don't question it."

This individual is also illiterate, functionally. He can read and knows Bible detail, but he is unable to reason out its application to life. When given an essay test that requires reasoning to a conclusion, he can't do it. He hates education because of its endless rote detail. He's not learning to think for himself under God.

Major goals in this education are proper behavior and authority sensitivity, a dependence on school and church structure, leaders and teachers. Discipline is based on external compliance, not internal character.

This improper fear of authority produces a slavish character in the individual, who deep down grows to feel a need for someone to control him. He can be manipulated due to a follow-the-leader mentality. This makes him vulnerable to cults, among other things. In the civil sphere, this dependence is shifted to the state, giving rise to dictatorship.

This is a swing in our sovereignty grid over to the right side where the structure is sovereign and governs a dependent people externally. On an airplane from Madrid, I once sat next to a lady who was starting private schools in Spain. Spain had had a stiff right-wing dictatorship and as she described public education there, it matched the right side of the sovereignty grid. Her private schools were a reaction to that education system and had swung to the left in the direction of our public schools with open classrooms, student-led education, experience-oriented learning centers and Values Clarification.

AMERICAN CHRISTIAN EDUCATION

The Biblical view that God is sovereign is represented in the center of the Sovereignty Grid for Education. This view produces an education to enhance internal government. This view was the basis of education leading up to America's founding that yielded the individual character necessary to produce and sustain liberty. There has been a refining and returning process in Christian education in America back in this direction in recent years. Here the child is seen not as just a "sensory being" or an "intellectual being" but as a "governing being." We are to teach our children to govern under God, making right choices. This involves not just emotions or mind, but focuses on will and character.[26]

This education is based on Bible understanding, not just Bible detail. The child is taught to recognize the hand of God in individuals' lives and events, discerning the "whys" of the Bible, not just the "whats." He learns to reason out true concepts from Biblical principles and apply them to every area of life. This will enable him to choose what is right and follow God in the midst of all the demands around him. He enjoys education because it has sense and purpose.[27]

True literacy consists not just in being able to read, but also in being able to apply what is read. It consists in knowing the Bible foundation and being able to reason from it to apply truth to every area of life. Not reading, not having a basis in truth, or not having a reasoning ability renders a person less than literate.

The goal is to form internally governed character, to teach the student to know how and why to govern himself under God. This person is not dependent on peers or authorities for what to do or think, but is independent. He cannot be manipulated. He is a leader not a follower, yet a servant not a dictator.

Another goal is to train self-educating character. This education teaches the student principles of research and trains him to apply those principles to his studies, whether Bible, history, government, language, math or science.

THE THIRD ALTERNATIVE IN EDUCATION

In summary, the autonomous character on the left needs external government because it is ungoverned. The dependent character on the right needs external government because of its dependence. Both give rise to tyranny. But the Biblical character is self-governed under God and non-dependent, giving rise to liberty. This was the educational philosophy pervasive in early America, when all education was done in the home and the church.

CHAPTER XIV.

HOW GOD CHANGES NATIONS

Five stages to transform a society.

To study the ways of God in changing a nation from tyranny to liberty, we will look at a nation in the Bible that God changed. As every person has a testimony of God's grace, every nation has a testimony of God's grace. The hand of God is at work in every nation to bless, to loose good and to restrain evil, thereby moving it towards liberty. Every nation can have liberty *if* the people will submit to His sovereignty.

The children of Israel went to Egypt as 70 persons (Gen. 46:27) and grew to approximately 3.5 million people by the time they left 430 years later. After some 300 years as slaves, their condition as a people was dismal as Landa Cope of Old Testament Template[28] points out. They were poor. They had no government. They had no work ethic. They had no economy. They had no land. They had a welfare mentality. They had no system of social order. They had no army. They had no visible means of support. They had no hygiene savvy or medical institutions. They had no scientific community. They had no agriculture. They had no industry. They had no religious system. They were the most undeveloped nation in history, before or since.

Yet God said, "I will make you the greatest nation on the face of the earth."

Years later, the Queen of Sheba came to visit Solomon and his kingdom to investigate a rumor she had heard of vast grandeur and blessing in Israel. She was aghast, saying in effect, "I hadn't heard the half of it!" (I Kin. 10:7).

165

They are an example for us.

The twelve sons of Israel had come to Egypt with their families in the midst of a famine as a result of God's work in one of them, Joseph. Joseph had the dubious privilege of thirteen years of misery in Egypt. First he was sold into slavery by his own brothers into the house of Potiphar, captain of the royal bodyguard (Gen. 37). Then he was unjustly accused by Potiphar's wife and thrown into Pharaoh's dungeons (Gen. 39-41). As Joseph remained a good and faithful servant in each situation, this time of trial equipped him for his next job as Pharaoh's chief officer in the kingdom. Joseph ultimately sent for his father and brothers and their families, and gave them all a place to settle in the land of Goshen, the best in Egypt, saving them from the famine.

What job is God training you for? If you don't know, neither did Joseph. He just trusted God and remained a good and faithful servant in the place where the Lord had him.

The twelve tribes of Israel grew in number and strength over four centuries. As foreigners, they were eventually set apart as laborers and finally enslaved. Being foreigners did, however, have the effect of keeping them a unified people, not assimilating into the Egyptian culture around them.

Exodus 1:8 says that another king rose to power who felt threatened by the sons of Israel. All he saw was a mass of people within his nation. In his insecurity he began to oppress the Israelites to intimidate them and keep them in their place as slaves. This had been foretold to Abraham years before.

> And God said to Abram, "Know for certain that your descendants will be strangers in a land that is not theirs, where they will be enslaved and oppressed four hundred years." Genesis 15:13

Exodus begins with the Pharaoh believing he is God and the Israelites having a mentality of total subordination to the state. For the most part, the people do not know God, although they have a heritage in Abraham the friend of God and a legend about the God of Abraham from 400 years before, that He would send a deliverer to deliver them. There was, however, a remnant that knew God and trusted Him with their lives.

> And the Lord said to Moses, "I have surely seen the affliction of My people who are in Egypt, and have given heed to their cry because of their taskmasters, for I am aware of their sufferings. So I have come down to deliver them from the power of the Egyptians..." Exodus 3:7-8

As the people cried out to God, He began to move in mercy to provide deliverance. It took 80 years for God to prepare His deliverer. Moses grew up as a grandson to Pharaoh. He was given the best education of the time and presumably was present while Pharaoh was wrestling with decisions of state until he was 40 years old. Then God took him to the desert for 40 years to learn the ways of the desert and to make him a good and faithful servant. By the time God was ready, Moses was the most humble man on earth (Num. 12:3).

Does your preparation seem slow? Moses would need that preparation considering the great wonders and revelations the Lord was about to give him. God knows our tendency to become proud with even just a pinch of truth. Moses was going to need all the humility, intellectual preparation and logistical wisdom that God was giving him.

At the proper time God released Moses into ministry, to deliver the sons of Israel out of Egypt to a place where they could get to know Him. The first stage in changing a nation is deliverance.

STAGE I - DELIVERANCE

God brings deliverance as the people of the land recognize their need and cry out to God in their distress, and as the people of God intercede for mercy. God will intervene on behalf of a nation if the people humble themselves in this way.

Consider Ninevah, "a great and wicked city" (Jon. 1:2). When God announced His impending judgement upon Ninivah for her violence, the people turned with such sincerity of repentance that they put even their animals in sackcloth and ashes. Their attitude was humility: "Perhaps God will turn and relent, and withdraw His burning anger so that we shall not perish?" God visited them in mercy upon seeing this and did not bring His intended judgment (Jon. 3:10). This means there is hope for the nations today.

God brought the people out of Egypt with great signs and wonders. Each of the plagues was against one of Egypt's gods, to show both His people and the people of Egypt that the Lord is the God of gods and alone deserves their allegiance. The final god of Egypt that was defeated was the state, as Pharaoh's army was drowned in the sea.

The sons of Israel left Egypt with a mentality of dependence on the state. Any people who does not know God is dependent on the state, dependent on external government for control. God now had to get the people to look up to Him, receive His law, and make an initial commitment to Him as their new King. The second stage of changing a nation is evangelism.

STAGE II - EVANGELISM

Evangelism consists of helping people look up to God, repent of their sins and place their faith in the Lord Jesus.

God revealed His awesome power to the people by the great signs and wonders He performed. He revealed His love for the people by bringing them out of their bondage and suffering in Egypt. He brought them up to the mountain and spoke to them:

> "You yourselves have seen what I did to the Egyptians, and how I bore you on eagles' wings, and brought you to Myself. Now then, if you will indeed obey My voice and keep My covenant, then you shall be My own possession among all the peoples, for all the earth is Mine; and you shall be to Me a kingdom of priests, and a holy nation." Ex. 19:4-6

The Lord God had their attention. On the basis of His power and love for them and His desire to govern them and bless them, they made their initial commitment to Him there in the desert.

> And all the people answered together and said,
> "All that the Lord has spoken we will do!" Ex. 19:8

When we make our initial commitment to the Lord Jesus, repent of our sins and self-centeredness, and trust Him to change us, transform us and lead us, we really have no idea of all that it will entail. But we have become basically convinced that God is good and loves us, that He has plans for us better than our own and that this is the best choice.

As we repent and make Him the center of our lives instead of ourselves, He begins a new work to teach us, transform us, protect us and conform us to His image.

> Therefore if any man is in Christ, he is a new
> creature; the old things passed away; behold, new
> things have come. II Cor. 5:17

The people in the desert really had no idea what this commitment would ultimately mean, but it was obvious to them the best option was to listen and obey.

As the people then crossed the desert towards the land of promise, still with the same self-centered and dependent character but following a new direction, they rebelled against God ten times (Num. 14:22), the first being while Moses was delayed in getting the Law from God on the mountain. After a few weeks, they figured it was over and made their own god, a golden calf. They said, "This is your god, O Israel, who brought you up from the land of Egypt," and worshipped it with a great feast (Ex. 32:1-6). Worshipping statues is what they had done in Egypt, and represented their lust for security, their ignorance of God and their rebellion.

Later, across the desert at the edge of the Promised Land at Kadesh-Barnea, their rebellion culminated when the twelve spies returned. Ten of them reported, "We are not able to take the land." Two of them, Joshua and Caleb pleaded, "If the Lord is pleased with us, He will bring us into the land!" The people rebelled, however, intending to go back to Egypt (Num. 14:1-4).

The people rebelled out of fear. Though they had seen God's works they had no faith, no strength of character, no will. The third stage of building a nation is discipleship.

STAGE III - DISCIPLESHIP

Discipleship is the process of building actual character in the individual that is faithful to God and self-governing under Him.

Character is the moral strength to resist temptation and do what is right without external force. The people of Israel had been delivered from bondage and had made an initial commitment to God the King. They must now become internally governed by their new King.

God's plan of blessing necessitated a shift in their character and mentality from the slavery mentality they had in Egypt to the freedom mentality they would need in the new land. This would take time. The Lord decided they would need 40 years in the wilderness.

The first aspect of this training was a shift from being a people who did not know God to being a people who knew God. We must know God in order to trust Him even when things are difficult or look bleak. We can see miracles, but that's not enough. Knowing God must be our primary personal activity and goal. This is what we were created for in the first place. Jeremiah said this:

> Thus says the Lord, "Let... him who boasts boast
> in this, that he knows and understands Me..." Jer.
> 9:23

God Himself wants us to know Him.

Looking back on this incident, Moses recalls the people saying, "Because the Lord hates us, He has brought us out of the land of Egypt to deliver us into the hand of the Amorites to destroy us!" (Deut. 1:27) But that was not why they were there. He was delivering them from slavery to liberty. They were there because He loved them! But they did not know Him so they did not trust Him.

There are many other aspects of this shift in character:

- From being self-serving to personal righteousness, from sinfulness to love. This creates moral strength and eliminates the tragic consequences of sin, individually and corporately.

170

- From being directionless to knowing God's voice. God has a plan and we must be able to discern the will of God for our lives, both in the major decisions and in the details.
- From being rebellious to being submissive. This is an attitude of unity, all going the same direction. A rebellious people is going each one his own way.
- From being fearful to taking initiative. This is the opposite of a slave mentality. It is recognizing what needs to be done and starting on one's own. There is no conflict here with submission, but all moving on their own together in unity.
- From being apathetic to being industrious. This means hard work. It will take hard work by everyone to build the nation.
- From being disloyal and haphazard to being faithful. Faithfulness is the basis of integrity in both personal relationships and corporate agreements.
- From being wasteful to being thrifty. This is being a faithful steward of all that God has provided and applying it to the task at hand. It includes time, money, relationships and assets.
- From a consumer character to a producer character. This is an active mentality of producing and building, not just soaking in and receiving.
- From a live-for-today mentality to living for future generations' blessing, not squandering what we have in assets, environment and health. It is a shift from living for immediate gratification to deferring for future fulfillment.
- From being self-centered to a character of love, living for the highest good of God and others instead of just personal happiness and advancement.
- From a character of dependence on the state to being dependent on God and self-controlled under Him.

From Slavery Character	To Freedom Character
Not knowing God	Knowing God
Selfishness	Righteousness
Sinfulness	Love
Directionless	Knowing God's voice
Fearfulness	Initiative
Apathy	Industry

Disloyalty	Faithfulness
Wastefulness	Thrift
Consumer	Producer
Living for today	Deferring for future fulfillment
Dependent on man and the state	Dependent on God

Fig. 14.1 Character Shift Necessary For Freedom.

The sons of Israel left Egypt with a slavery character of weakness. To enter Canaan and maintain liberty they would need a new freedom character of strength.

This transformation is happening in many nations and peoples today as revivals of the past few decades have settled into discipleship movements, training Christian character in the multitudes who have been coming to Christ. The generation who came out of Egypt spent the next 40 years learning and hammering out these things in their own lives and then training their children. The next stage of building a nation is education.

STAGE IV - EDUCATION

True education consists in transferring Godly character and Biblical wisdom forward to the next generation. The sons of Israel are commanded by God to teach the next generation as a main concern:

> "And all these words, which I am commanding you today, shall be on your heart; and you shall teach them diligently to your sons and shall talk of them when you sit in your house and when you walk in the way and when you lie down and when you rise up..." Deut. 6:4-9

The task and responsibility of education belongs to the family. This represents a vastly decentralized system of education. Parents may delegate this task to others, but final accountability rests with them. Delegating this task to others still requires involvement by parents, in fact more involvement as the school gets farther from the parents' Biblical values.

This education is not just academic, but concerns Christian character. Any old education will not do. Education that produces autonomous character will yield an ungoverned and ungovernable population who need strong external force for control. Education that produces dependent character will yield people who feel the need for control and guidance. Either way, this dependence erodes freedom.

The parent generation that came out of Egypt spent much of their time and energy unlearning their old ways and habits and learning this new freedom character. The next generation learned it from them from birth, growing up with a new character of dependence on God. They had not been steeped in slavery all their lives but were able to start fresh. When they approached the Jordan River 40 years later, they looked at it overflowing its banks and wondered, "What is the Lord going to do now?" The Lord told them to get up and march towards the swollen river. They did so and when their feet touched the water, God parted it for them (Josh. 3:1-7). I imagine myself among them and wonder what I would have been thinking at the time, or if I would have joined their column at all! This was truly a people of different character than those who left Egypt.

When Fidel Castro came to power he sent teachers throughout Latin America. This was touted as a great humanitarian gesture, raising the literacy level of the people. But they were also training a character of subordination to the state, the pagan view of man, for future adventures. The church has taught this dependence as well. While distributing Bibles in Mexico I spoke with a lady who told me, "Oh no. I can't read the Bible. The priest reads the Bible and tells me what it says." This is dependence on a church structure for knowledge of God instead of on the Bible. Many Protestants also fail to read their Bibles, but depend on the weekly sermon for spiritual growth. This laziness also represents dependent character. People also depend on the church structure for forgiveness and guidance instead of the Lord. This gives power to the structure, and when it becomes excessive it can become a cult.

As the sons of Israel crossed the Jordan they faced new challenges: the ceasing of the manna (Josh. 5:12), the walls of Jerico (Josh. 6:16-20), the inhabitants of the land (Josh. 11:16-20). In each of these new challenges they had to trust God and seek Him for new solutions. The next stage is to apply what they had learned in the wilderness in building the nation.

STAGE V - BUILDING THE NATION

Building your nation is a matter of being salt and light as Jesus admonished us, applying Biblical wisdom to every area of life (Matt. 5:13-16).

The generation of the sons of Israel that entered the Land had the character they needed to sustain liberty without a human king. They had what they needed to follow God's lead, move into the land and build a nation. The nation was first built internally, then externally. God warned them to be careful to keep priorities in that order:

> "This book of the law shall not depart from your mouth, but you shall meditate on it day and night, so that you may be careful to do according to all that is written in it; for then you will make your way prosperous, and then you will have success." Josh. 1:8

God brought them into the land, but it took a lot of work to build the nation. It did not happen in a single day or a single year, but as they were faithful, following the Lord closely in their personal lives, their families and their relationships together, they took the land.

All of these stages are going on in nations at the same time: Prayer, Evangelism, Discipleship, Christian Education, Building. God emphasizes different stages in different nations at different times as God sees the need and as His people respond to His call. That is why we cannot look down on a people for not understanding the basic parts of Biblical economics if God is teaching them prayer and evangelism.

It takes time to build character and a new mentality in a people, even for God. A pastor said to me, "That will take forever!" No, it only takes a generation or two, but if we don't start now, it won't happen. There is no other way to secure liberty. As I was praying one day about this time frame, the Lord directed me to a scripture that was the word of the Lord to Isaiah:

> "Can a land be born in one day?
> Can a nation be brought forth all at once?
> As soon as Zion travailed, she also brought forth her
>   sons.
> "Shall I bring to the point of birth, and not give
>   delivery?" says the Lord.
> Or shall I who gives delivery shut the womb?" says
>   your God. Is. 66:8-9

No, a land cannot be built in one day, but yes, this is what God is doing. God compares the process to the travailing cacophony of a baby being born. It is easy to assume that since God is doing it, it will be easy and fall into place. This is a mentality of apathy brought about by peace and ease. We must seek God to change our character, "beginning with me!"

Paul says, "There are no odd parts of the body" (I Cor. 12:12 LB). In the body of Christ we each have a significant place of service in one or more of these stages. Our task is to seek Him to find what that place is, and be faithful to Him as He teaches us how best to apply our gifts and talents.

CHAPTER XV.

STEWARDS OF SOCIETY

"Well done, good and faithful servant, enter into thy rest."

When the sons of Israel began to move into the land of promise, Joshua went out to survey the city of Jericho, whose "walls were high and whose doors were shut tight" (Josh. 6:1). The Bible records a most extraordinary event in Joshua 5:13-15. "And behold a man was standing opposite him with his sword drawn in his hand, and Joshua went up to him and said to him, 'Are you for us or for our adversaries?'" The man facing Joshua had a most interesting and succinct answer, "No." He added, "Rather I indeed come now as captain of the host of the Lord." By saying this he indicated that he was from another realm, representing a different kingdom. "No," he said. He was for neither "us" nor "them" but God was doing something new. The sons of Israel were going to need more than their muscle and their wits to accomplish what God had in mind for them. They would also need the "host of the Lord." Their job would be simply to obey the Lord in detail in their lives, and He would bring about an incredible victory. One can infer from this event that God is not particularly interested in our squabbles, but in our faithfulness and obedience to Him. The center of the universe is neither them nor us, but Him!

God the Creator is involved in a long-term endeavor to establish His kingdom among men. He "so loved the world that He gave His only begotten Son that whosoever believes on Him might not perish but have life everlasting" (John 3:16). Jesus taught us that we should pray for His kingdom to come. The wonderful result of the kingdom of God is great blessing and peace. The King Himself is the source of love, peace and forgiveness. God is interested in changing chaotic and needy nations to places of freedom, order, safety and prosperity. Why? That the nations might have a testimony of His goodness and grace. Yet, if God is going to change and bless the nations, we His people must each take our own individual part seriously. And we each have a part. There are no "odd parts" of the body of Christ. Each of us is significant in the scope of His plans and each of us has vital contributions to make.

The essence of this discussion has been the kingdom of God within each believer, an internal kingdom. Jesus is the King of kings and the Lord of lords (I Tim. 6:15), the top authority in heaven and on earth (Matt. 28:18). To the degree that people govern themselves within His authority, there is freedom. The concept of "stewardship of society" refers to a sense of responsibility to apply what God has given us to every aspect of life in order to multiply His blessings.

In Bible times, a steward was a servant who took care of his master's affairs while his master was away. The Bible tells us, "The earth is the Lord's and the fullness thereof" (Ps. 24:1). Those who know Him, therefore, are the stewards of planet earth, of society and, in our discussion, of civil government. Unfortunately, we have allowed in our day the idea of stewardship to be greatly diminished to the mere process of financing the local church. As the body of Christ we must regain from the Lord by the Holy Spirit His vision for us for the stewardship of society. Jesus tells us the necessity of faithfulness in the stewardship of what He has given us (Luke 12:42-48).

As far as God's motivation goes, Jesus came that we might have life and have it "more abundantly" (John 10:10). He has bestowed among us many various talents and gifts. His instructions to His disciples, and therefore to us, were to "occupy" until He returns. We don't know when that will be but we must utilize what He has given us until He does and be ready for His return at any time. We must not be "wicked and lazy" servants of His (Matt. 25:26), sitting on the abilities He has given us, "hiding our lamps under bushels" (Matt. 5:14-16).

The Bible is in reality the ideological foundation of the entirety of Western culture in general and the American civil structure in particular. Kenneth Woodward, writing for Newsweek magazine, made this statement: "But by any secular standard, Jesus is the dominant figure of Western culture. Like the millennium itself, much of what we now think of as Western ideas, inventions and values finds its source or inspiration in the religion that worships God in his name. Art and science, the self and society, politics and economics, marriage and the family, right and wrong, body and soul - all have been touched and often radically transformed by Christian influence."[29] As such, it is of critical importance that we understand that the task of the maintenance of the American culture and civil structure belongs to Biblical people. Otherwise our culture will be increasingly dominated by sensuality, selfishness and materialism and our civil structure will collapse.

But it is more than just a task, a mere nod to Judeo-Christian values, or so-called "family values." It is a vital personal responsibility. We have lost this mentality in the church as we have strayed from relationship with the living Jesus to a static and formalistic religion in the midst of a determined quest for material things.

This sense of stewardship responsibility in the area of civil government has devolved over the years to simple political action or mere rhetoric, or for many Christians to nothing at all. We are reaping the consequences of this inaction within our land as a result. Stewardship is not about control, but about helping, serving, leading, choosing, governing, blessing and being an example. Civil government is part of our stewardship because civil government is a divine institution. It exists for the purpose of protecting the natural rights given to us by God and must be kept within that boundary in order to be a blessing to the people and not a curse. A fire is a blessing in a fire ring or fireplace, but not on the living room floor. Fire has a proper and appropriate place. We must not ignore such a vital part of our stewardship as civil government.

"GETTING POLITICAL"

Therefore, now is the time for all of God's people to "get political." But we must do it properly. Getting political simply means shaking off the apathy and exercising our stewardship in the sphere of civil government.

Jesus instructed us to be wise and harmless (Matt. 10:16). I take this to mean actually wise and actually harmless, without another agenda. We are representing His kingdom. Our political mentality must be to ensure the highest good and a future. This participation in civil government is not a side issue for Christians, but an integral part of loving our neighbors as ourselves, seeking their highest good as well as our own. Nor is "getting political" *the* central issue, but rather one more aspect of life to keep in proper balance. God will help us, through His word and Spirit, to keep properly focused on His kingdom, not men's kingdoms. In fact He says, "Your ears will hear a word behind you saying, 'This is the way, walk ye in it,' whenever you turn to the right or to the left," (Is. 30:21).

What is the practical application of the responsibility to "get political?" Getting political does *not* mean simply voting Christians into office in the next election, and breathing a sigh of relief. It does not mean setting up an external Christian legal structure to control the people. Getting political does not mean trusting in civil government to solve the peoples' problems. It does not mean compromising with the world's system of greed and control, and the "factional scheming for power and status" of politics.

What, then, does it mean for us as Christians to "get political?" It simply means to learn to think "governmentally" with respect to the ramifications of the lordship of Christ, the kingdom of God, in our day. It means specifically to learn to govern ourselves in the civil sphere of life. We don't need fanfare to go about affecting our world. We just need faithfulness. And we must all take part, "encouraging one another to love and good works" (Heb. 10:24), seeking the Lord for specifics.

"Getting political" refers to adding Biblical principles of civil government and economics to our concept of discipleship, and to our mentality, with proper emphasis. It includes the recognition that as the church, we should be continually helping the poor and working to eliminate poverty. It means that as believers, we educate our children in order to eliminate ignorance and dependent character.

"Getting political" does not necessarily require expending vast amounts of time and energy. It does, however, mean expending *some* portion of our time and energy learning about civil government, becoming informed, strategizing, voting, supporting good candidates, thinking through principles, making application to specific issues and educating others.

Given the foundation of sound internal government, as outlined previously, the task is then to maintain a sound external civil government. We do this by electing people of integrity and intelligence into public office at every level and monitoring them intelligently and with humility. Vigilance is active stewardship. We need to pray, find quality people and help them get into office. Then we must give them the benefit of studied Biblical wisdom and input to help them lead well.

People who would make a career in government service need to possess a comprehensive Biblical worldview. Elected officials, and their staff workers, need to understand the genuine difference between right and wrong and not simply proceed with current thoughts and opinions as their sole guide. It is imperative that politicians recognize the high intrinsic value of the individual and the equality of value of all individuals in order to govern justly. They should exemplify honesty and humility; they should be people who can be trusted. They must recognize that the proper purpose and function of civil government is protection, not control. They must be people of proven character who will be able to resist corruption because before all else they lead by example, especially in this media age. Those who are corrupt will lead by example towards lawlessness.

OR "DEMANDING A KING"

"Getting political" does not mean demanding a king.

A major problem with our generation is that as we have gotten used to and come to enjoy, even take for granted, the good *things* God has given us, we have drifted away from *Him*. We are demanding a king to take care of us on every hand – in civil government, in economics, in education, in our personal lives, even in our church leadership. We want a king to fight our battles for us and provide for us. Even as Christians, we want a king to control the world around us. If we are not careful, if we do not turn back to Him, He may very well give us our king. We will soon "cry out because of the procedure of the king who reigns over [us], but the Lord will not answer

[us] in that day" (I Sam. 8:18). Now is the time to take seriously Jesus' admonition to repent for the kingdom of God is at hand.

That is the first step – repentance. We must turn from living for ourselves as our purpose in life to living for God and others as our purpose in life. We must choose anew to stop living for our own happiness and personal gain to live for God and His purposes for our lives and for our world.

EZRA'S BLUEPRINT

Ezra was one of those Jews who returned from the Babylonian captivity to rebuild Jerusalem and his nation. In simple form, the mechanism to bring about his effective stewardship is summarized:

> The good hand of his God was upon him, for Ezra had set his heart to study the law of the Lord, and to practice it, and to teach His statutes and ordinances in Israel. Ezra 7:10

The scriptural keys, then, are studying, practicing and teaching the ways of God. These principles have not changed since Ezra's time. "His good hand" will be upon us if we will do the same.

Christian scholarship is the standard to which God's people must attain in our day. We must learn the principles of liberty if we are to know what to do to be free. Practicing them is essential for us to truly understand how to apply these principles to build the foundations of a free society. Teaching these principles to others is essential if we are to be free together as a people. Teaching them to the next generation is necessary so that our children and future generations can enjoy the blessings of freedom as well.[30] Teaching these principles to the nations is our stewardship responsibility in God's purpose in history, as Jesus commissioned us.

EZRA STUDIED THE LAW OF THE LORD

As the children of Israel were about to enter the land He had promised, the Lord admonished the people through Joshua:

"Only be strong and courageous to be careful to
do according to all the law which Moses My servant
commanded you; do not turn from it to the right or
to the left, so that you may have success wherever
you go. This book of the law shall not depart from
your mouth, but you shall meditate on it day and
night, so that you may be careful to do according to
all that is written in it, for then you will make your
way prosperous, and then you will have success."
Josh. 1:7-8

The people were directed to study the book of the law, to meditate on God's word day and night. This would keep their focus on
the Lord God and give them understanding of what they were to do
on an everyday basis in order to prosper and succeed. This would
not be a burden to them, but a blessing that would permeate their
lives, individually and corporately. The "book of the law" taught the
big picture of God's purpose for them and also the immediate
picture of their daily lives, relationships and choices. Likewise, *we*
also must study God's word continually. One hour on Sunday
morning is not enough.

The Bible has the answers to every aspect of our lives. We
desperately need to gain God's vantage point from which to view our
relationships, our surroundings, our institutions and our world. The
Bible imparts to us understanding both of God's sovereignty and His
multiplicity of purposes. The former will give us hope and the latter
outlines our responsibility, which will lead us to true freedom.

PRACTICAL STUDY LIFESTYLE

Developing a personal Bible study and devotional time is of
primary importance. The purpose of life is to know God (John
17:3). Reserving a time regularly, daily if possible, to spend with
Him in prayer and studying the Bible will help us learn who He
really is and how to build our relationship with Him.

Ask the Holy Spirit to illuminate His word. Apply what He
teaches you. This is holiness. Adopt a daily reading plan to read
through the Bible each year. Keep at it for the rest of your life.

Research your personal study fascinations and topics of interest to you. Learn to use Bible resources to enhance your study. Think through the applications of what you find. Keep a journal of what the Lord teaches you. Adopt a Scripture memory plan. Develop your personal prayer list. There are also many other good books that can help you develop your relationship with God.

Secondly, think through the concepts and principles. What does it mean that we are made in the image of God? What does it mean that all individuals are of equal value intrinsically? How do I live that way? What are Biblical principles of government and how do they apply to my life and mentality? What does it mean that God is sovereign, not the church or the state, and not the individual? What should my mentality and choices be considering the principle that in reality there is no class structure, "neither Jew nor Greek, bond nor free, male nor female, for you are all one in Christ Jesus" (Gal. 3:28)? Why is submitting to God's government intelligent?

What principles of <u>civil</u> government can we reason from the Scriptures? Of <u>family</u> government? What are contrasting ideas? How do I implement these things personally, and in my society?

Third, relate these principles to the various issues of the day reasoning how Biblical principles define the issues. Most of our discussion about issues is typically opinions, feelings and preferences, not the principles that actually define the issues. The result is chaos, not stability, "every man doing what is right in his own eyes" (Judg. 21:25).

Fourth, study Biblical principles of government in your Bible study group or Sunday school class. Group study is valuable to 'hash over' the ideas with others.

Fifth, become informed and keep abreast of current events. Read the newspaper and/or a news magazine to keep up on world events and local events of the day. Invest time praying for the needs and problems. Identify Biblical principles in the articles. What is really happening and why? What will the result be? What would the Biblical solution be? Write well-reasoned letters to your representatives and newspaper editor to help them understand the issues and solutions. Approach them with humility and a motive to help them, not force them. Have a friend help you refine and edit your letters for clarity and tone.

It is important to understand the concepts and principles thoroughly and be able to convey them clearly to someone else in a sound, rational and humble way. Practice communicating the principles within your sphere of influence. If Biblical principles of government become part of the discipleship of this generation of Christians, the world will be a different place in generations to come.

EZRA PRACTICED THE LAW OF THE LORD

Once you have discerned a course of action to be the will of God, practice it faithfully. "Only be courageous to *do*" (Josh. 1:7).

Our first job, then, is practicing holiness, which is simply staying away from personal sin. Sin always works against relationships, with God and with others.

Then comes obedience to the principles and directives the Lord gives in His word. We study the scriptures to find out what to do, and then we do it in the spirit of Jesus, which is love. We must make right choices in our lives to reap consequences that are good. If we choose what is wrong, we will reap bad consequences. Some consequences may surface years later, but they result from our choices now.

On a large scale the broader need is for true spiritual awakening, but on the immediate scale the need concerns me, a simple individual. People tend to think of the government as "them," something outside. In reality the government is "we," or more specifically "me." Therefore, my own character is what my first project must be, taking on responsibility in every area of my daily life. These responsibilities include relationships with others, especially my marriage and my family, and my integrity in all areas of life and endeavor. This will be a long-term learning and growing process. We must resist a quick-fix mentality in character building.

Perhaps the most important task I must accomplish is making sure my marriage is rooted in the Lordship of Christ. My marriage is the first place in life that I have to die to self and live for someone else's happiness and fulfillment. Divorce comes when someone becomes mired in self-centeredness. The shameful rate of divorce among people who claim to be believers in Christ is speaking to our culture that there really is no hope. This trend must end by the grace of God.

My next most important task concerns raising my own children. It is not the job of the state or the school to raise my children. This task is not to be relinquished to day care centers, baby sitters, televisions, computer games, Hollywood, or even the church youth group. I must raise my children. No one else. And the only way to do that is to *be there*. This will mean giving up the quest to "keep up with the Joneses," ceasing to make the accumulation of material goods my main priority in life. It may mean a change in career. It may mean pulling back in ministry. It may mean a smaller house. The proper balance must be struck so our children are not abandoned to grow up on their own. Abdicating this responsibility will bring about dire consequences. As Christian parents, if we allow forces and influences other than ourselves to raise the next generation, our society will continue to move towards anarchy and violence. "Being afraid of your own children is a terrible judgement," one concerned mother told me recently. This breakdown is a consequence of ignoring God's priorities. The result will be a descent to tyranny.

Vocation is next. The word "vocation" means "calling." God has given us gifts and callings. Vocation involves recognizing from the Lord what His calling is, and then doing it as unto Him, whatever it may be. Because my life is of real value, my work, which is the use of a portion of my life, is also of real value. That is why I can be remunerated for my labor. We are to govern ourselves to maximize the value of our work and time.

Mixed in are other areas of stewardship and life, caring for the needy, helping other believers and expanding the kingdom.

EZRA TAUGHT THE LAW OF THE LORD

The sons of Israel were made a nation and a culture by Moses' teaching. Moses had spoken to them as they were preparing to enter Canaan.

> "And these words, which I am commanding you
> today, shall be on your heart; and you shall teach
> them diligently to your sons and shall talk of them
> when you sit in your house and when you walk by

the way and when you lie down and when you rise up." Deut. 6:6

Then he warned them not to forget the Lord God.

> "Beware lest you forget the Lord your God by not keeping His commandments...lest when you have eaten and are satisfied and have built good houses and lived in them... then your heart becomes proud, and you forget the Lord your God who brought you out from the land of Egypt, out of the house of slavery...
>
> "And it shall come about that if you ever forget the Lord your God, and go after other gods and serve and worship them, I testify against you today that you shall surely perish." Deut. 8:11,20

The third generation in Canaan, however, began to fall apart. "There arose another generation after them who did not know the Lord, nor yet the work which He had done for Israel" (Judg. 2:7-11). The result of forgetting what God had done for them was that "they forsook the Lord, the God of their fathers." Here was a generation that had *not been taught* the ways and acts of God. Their freedom turned to anarchy as they lost sight of the Lord God.

The kingdom of God is also a culture unified by the teaching of the Scriptures. Jesus said in His last address to His disciples, "Go, therefore, and make disciples of all the nations, baptizing them in the name of the Father, the Son and the Holy Spirit, teaching them all that I have commanded you" (Matt. 28:19). Wycliff and the other reformers believed that if we teach the Bible to the people, society would be built from within. There is a sense in this Great Commission scripture in which we are all called to teach, in addition to those who are specifically called and gifted to be teachers in the body of Christ. The idea is "each one teach one."

As we are faithful with the depth of our lives, which is character, God will take care of the breadth of our lives, which is influence. As we spend time developing our relationship with Jesus, seeking Him diligently, studying His word and putting into practice what He teaches us, the Lord will open doors for us to teach others. We can only bring others as far in the Lord as we have come ourselves.

ELECTED OFFICE

The external component of our stewardship of society with respect to civil government here in America concerns the individuals who are in elected office. Representatives at every level are making decisions each day that affect our lives. They make these critical decisions based on their own presuppositions, personal character – whether noble or greedy – and a vast array of information inputs from various sources. These people need our prayer. The future is not in any one human's hands alone. Leaders need prayer for conviction of truth and wisdom. Civil government is a joint venture between God, us and our leaders.

We must be energetic and committed enough to release individuals into public office who will keep civil government confined to its proper mission and task, not expanding into areas in which it does not belong. The first job of our representatives is to govern the civil government.

It is plain, then, that we need to vote. In order to ensure quality representation, the first requirement for us is to cast an informed vote. This is a matter of our character as well. If we as Christians do not have enough Godly character to vote intelligently for those who are to represent us in civil government, then authority over our lives will shift upwards and we and our children will lose our freedom. As power shifts upwards, corruption increases. Neglecting to vote defends corruption; this is not the will of God.

We need to vote and get other believers to vote, teaching them why to vote. We need to strategize based on the highest good and future of our communities, cities, states and nation. The direction, purpose and quality of the decisions of our public servants will be defined by their worldview, character, intelligence and experience.

We also need to be willing to respond to the Lord's calling if He wants us to run for office ourselves. If we should attain to the privilege of elected office, we must govern with the wisdom and insight of His ways. There are many positions in civil government at local, state and national levels that need good and wise people to serve as representatives. One could begin with becoming a precinct commit-tee worker, moving up to school board, city council, county board, state legislature and further, learning everything possible at each level. Faithfulness in the small things will bring about advance to greater things. The lower levels of government are actually the more important as they have the most immediate impact on the individual's life.

The idea of stewardship implies a continuous process of learn-ing and taking on responsibility. We should be growing in more and more areas of understanding, resisting discouragement and continu-ally looking to Jesus. The Biblical concept of responsibility in the stewardship of society is the same for every nation, though specific opportunities to exercise that stewardship may differ.

CAUTION

The various components of Christian self-government presented in this book must be kept in proper balance together. Governing myself under God means governing myself according to law *and* love. God's law is the Law of Love. Spiritual maturity means becoming more like Jesus, not more like the Pharisees.

Christian self-government is marked by compassion and mercy, characterized by helping others. All too easily, our mentality can shift to "I'm taking on my responsibility, now you take on yours. You need to get your life together and pull yourself up by your own bootstraps. Be warmed and filled." Rather we must help others grow in taking on responsibility, getting their lives together and becoming fulfilled and productive citizens of God's kingdom. This is investing our lives in individual people who have needs - spiri-tual, physical and social. This is loving our neighbor as ourselves.

Paul might say, "I can take on all kinds of responsibility and govern myself in every area of life, but if I have not love it is harsh and sterile, clanging symbols and noisy brass."

The Pilgrims in Plymouth, believing that Christian self-govern-ment was the form and spirit of their new colony, saw that both integrity and compassion were the colony's spiritual foundations. Those in England who financed their voyage had promised to replenish them with food and tools and supplies from time to time.

What they in fact did was bring shiploads of destitute people, without bringing the promised supplies and tools and seed. Instead of pointing these people down the road to hack out their own way as they had done, the Pilgrims took them in, taught them, cared for them and helped them so they could make it, too. This was at no small expense to themselves personally. But they saw that love was to rule, not personal comfort and gain. Also, though financed at 40% interest, they eventually paid off their debt with interest.

The letter kills but the Spirit gives life (II Cor. 3:6). We must take care continuously to keep Jesus in the center of our lives, not just correct government. We may have correct external forms, but without the internal guts of the love of God, and Jesus Himself who is "the way, the truth and the life" (John 14:6), even our correct forms will tend to veer off into oppression. To keep this proper balance, we need continuing personal spiritual awakening and repentance without which we shift in our hearts towards license and dependence.

SOVEREIGNTY OF GOD

The Reformation brought out a resurgence of the idea that God is sovereign in the individual's life, not the individual himself and not the church nor the state. If a people will govern themselves under Him, they can be free without spawning chaos. Since Reformation times the Bible has spread exponentially throughout the world. God has a plan. It is a long-term plan and He is accomplishing it.

We must believe in the sovereignty of God, and individually do what He has given us to do. He has a destiny for the nations and has commissioned us to be part of it. His kingdom is expanding faster than ever before. There is real hope in Jesus! We each need to walk in that hope. "If the Lord is pleased with us, then He will bring us into this land, and give it to us - a land which flows with milk and honey" (Num. 14:8). The kingdom of God is Jesus' lordship in our lives. We have no king but Jesus. "His kingdom ruleth over all," (Ps. 103:19).

The structures exist to serve Him and bless us. Civil government in its various spheres is an institution bestowed on man by

God. It is to be designed and maintained to accomplish its divine purpose of protecting the individual, encouraging the good and restricting the evil. And it is His people who are charged with being faithful stewards of this institution until He returns.

RESOURCES

JUDAH BIBLE CURRICULUM

As **an educational companion to this book,** the author has compiled a Bible curriculum for Bible class K-12 in Christian schools and home schools, Sunday schools and personal study. The Judah Bible Curriculum is a "Principle Approach" Bible class curriculum based on the Biblical philosophy of government in the center column of the Education Sovereignty Grid, Chapter XIII. It is a Bible study, not a study about the Bible, helping you to teach your students principles of research and reasoning skills so that they will not grow up to be dependent in character. In order for us and our children to make it and flourish in our world today, we must know the Bible. This curriculum is being used by parents and schools to cult-proof and peer-proof their children, and train them for real freedom with Godly restraint.

For further information, visit us on the web at
www.JudahBible.com or write to:

Judah Bible Curriculum
P.O. Box 122
Urbana, IL, 61803

ENDNOTES

[1] Hall, Verna M. and Slater, Rosalie J. *The Bible and the Constitution*, San Francisco, Foundation for American Christian Education, 1983, p.14.

[2] Webster, Noah, *An American Dictionary of the English Language, 1828*, reprinted by Foundation for American Christian Education, 1980.

[3] Kurtz, Paul ed., *Humanist Manifestos I and II*, Prometheus Books, 1973, p. 8.

[4] *Ibid.* p. 17.

[5] Slater, Rosalie J. *Teaching and Learning America's Christian History*, San Francisco, Foundation for American Christian Education, 1965, p. 334.

[6] *Ibid.* p. 336

[7] *Ibid.* pp. 336-337.

[8] Hall, Verna M. *The Christian History of the Constitution of the United States of America, Christian Self-Government*, San Francisco, Foundation for American Christian Education, 1966, pp. 191-193, Of Plymouth Plantation.

[9] *Ibid.* p. 204. Mayflower Compact.

[10] *Ibid.* p. 204.

[11] *Ibid.* p. 206.

[12] *Ibid.* p. 213.

[13] *Ibid.* p. 213.

[14] *Ibid.* p. 215.

[15] *Ibid.* p. 346B. Declaration of Independence.

[17] Madison, James, "Property," 1792, *The Christian History of the Constitution of the United States of America, Christian Self-Government*, p. 248A.

[18] Webster, Noah, *An American Dictionary of the English Language, 1828*.

[19] Washington, George, *George Washington Papers at the Library of Congress, 1741-1799*, Series 3h Varick Transcripts, Internet image and transcription.

[20] Grant, George, *Bringing in the Sheaves, Transforming Poverty into Productivity*, American Vision Press, 1985, p. 118. Bringing in the Sheaves is an excellent practical manual for the church on how to eliminate poverty.

[21] Anderson, Fenwick, "Cousins Says World Government Needed to Solve Global Problems", *The Daily Illini*, 4/20/77, Urbana, Illinois, p. A6.

[22] *Humanist Manifestos I and II*, p. 21.

[23] This section is a summary of an excellent article by Charles Hull Wolf entitled "The Principle Approach to American Christian Economics" published in *A Guide to American Christian Education* by James B. Rose, American Christian History Institute, 1987, pp. 393-424.

[24] DoSoto, Hernando, *The Other Path*, The Invisible Revolution in the Third World, Harper & Row, 1989. The Other Path proposes freeing these underground economies so they can flourish.

[25] An excellent video series by Milton Friedman entitled *Free To Choose* compares the economies of India and Hong Kong. Available from PBS. org.

[26] This type of education is being re-pioneered today in America and is called Principle Approach education.

[27] *The Judah Bible Curriculum* is a Principle Approach Bible curriculum for studying the Bible in this way. It is for use in Christian schools and home schools, Sunday school classes, and personal study. Written by Bill Burtness. See www.JudahBible.com.

[28] See www.OTTemplate.org,

[29] Woodward, Kenneth, "2000 Years of Jesus," *Newsweek*, March 29, 1999, lead article.

[30] See *The Judah Bible Curriculum*, Resources, P. 199.

Printed in the United States
64162LVS00007B/217

9 781591 602323